NAIL YOUR NARRATIVE

How to use storytelling to reinvent your career in midlife

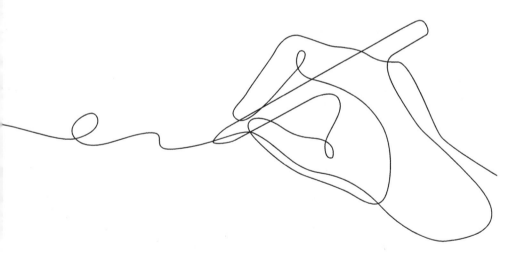

SARAH BIRD

Nail Your Narrative

Copyright © 2025 by Sarah Lesley Bird
Copyright © all photographs by Poppy Jakes

All rights reserved. No part of this book may be reproduced or transmitted in any form or by any means, electronic or mechanical, including photocopying, recording, or by any information storage and retrieval system, without written permission from the author, except for the inclusion of brief quotations in a review.

The author and the contributors are not responsible for any consequences resulting from the use or misuse of the information provided.

Disclaimer of Endorsement: The mention or reference of any specific products, services, or organisations in this book does not constitute an endorsement or recommendation by the author or publisher. The inclusion of such references is solely for informational purposes and should not be construed as an endorsement of their quality, suitability, or effectiveness. Readers are encouraged to conduct research and make informed decisions based on their needs and preferences. The author and contributors disclaim any liability for the actions or outcomes resulting from using any mentioned products, services, or organisations.

Cover Design: Alex Bird and Kinga Stabryla
Photography: Poppy Jakes Photography
Editing: Kinga Stabryla
Proofreading: Kinga Stabryla

First Edition: 2025
ISBN 978-1-0686479-3-2

Published with the support of Brandspire Digital Limited, United Kingdom, https://brandspire.co.uk

Printed in the United Kingdom

DEDICATION

To my son, Alex, with love and thanks
for being the best of my story

Contents

CHAPTER 1
CONFESSIONS OF A STORYTELLER   9

CHAPTER 2
WORK—THE LAST TABOO?   13

CHAPTER 3
MIDLIFE MAYHEM   25

CHAPTER 4
WHAT MIDLIFE JOBSEEKERS SHOULD KNOW   39

CHAPTER 5
WHAT MIDLIFE EMPLOYEES SHOULD KNOW   61

CHAPTER 6
THE ROLE OF THE NARRATIVE   75

CHAPTER 7
HOW TO GET STARTED 91

CHAPTER 8
FUTURE-PROOF RESILIENCE 95

CHAPTER 9
FIVE STEPS TO NAIL YOUR NARRATIVE 107

CHAPTER 10
SUCCESSFUL STORIES 117

Acknowledgements 121

Further reading 123

Endnotes 125

About the author 129

No time to read these days?

Reading aids include:

 JUMP to suggestions for linked or relevant content.

 QUICK FIX chapter summaries for headline takeaways.

 WORKBOOK TIP guiding you to relevant exercises to explore your own thinking.

 TRY NOW useful ways you can translate this content today.

Keen to get started?

This book aims to demonstrate the benefits of applying Narrative Practice to explore your goals, behaviours and attitudes to find a new way to be more ready and resilient in the workplace.

If you'd like to put what you are reading into practice, take a moment to download the accompanying Workbook. It's split into four easy-to-follow sections with 24 practical exercises to get you up and running with nailing your narrative. Visit www.nynclub.co.uk to access your free copy.

CHAPTER 1

CONFESSIONS OF A STORYTELLER

Let's start with a story and seed the idea that storytelling can be a powerful technique in crafting your midlife career transformation.

I'm going to confess this up front so you all know where I stand. It's one of those admissions that some people might think I should keep to myself. But since this book is about telling stories, then it's highly relevant. I wouldn't call it a dirty little secret, more something of a guilty pleasure. And I'm not alone.

I am a huge fan of Hallmark-Channel-style movies. Phew, said it! Let me explain for the uninitiated. There's a certain formula to a Hallmark movie, especially when it comes to the subject matter of Christmas. I'll set the scene for you.

There's a single woman somewhere in the United States—let's say New York. She's a career woman with no time for men/dating. All her friends and family feel she works too hard. She's driven and may (or may not) realise there's something missing in her life.

With news of the death of an estranged relative who owns a quaint but dilapidated retail shop in the wholesome leafy idyll of Vermont, she's asked to go and sort out the sale—she's keen to do this fast as her stellar, demanding career is waiting back in New York.

But wait! There happens to be a handsome, single widower who's bringing up his cute seven-year-old daughter on his own who has been valiantly running the shop—and all the friendly, welcoming townsfolk are keen for it to stay open. Skip to a reveal that city life isn't all it's cracked up to be, the single woman finds her eminently suitable prince and turns out to be the perfect stepmom, and everyone lives happily ever after. Oh yes, and let's not forget, it's Christmas, so in the last frame, there's snow.

Still with me? You can tell I've seen A LOT of these movies. There's something in the repeatable rhythm of the story, the inevitable resolution, that I find both enjoyable and comforting—and based on the number of movies with this storyline out there, it's clearly a successful formula.

So what do Hallmark movies have to do with your midlife career? More than you may think. Underneath the predictable plotlines and perfectly packaged endings lies something fundamental and universal—**the power of the narrative.** Through their recognisable storylines, these movies tap into outcomes we all desire: clarity, purpose, and a sense of fulfilled destiny in how our own story unfolds. And while real life doesn't come with a guaranteed happy ending, we *can* control the story we tell about ourselves, especially when it comes to our working lives.

We spend an awful lot of time at work. One published study found that the average person will spend 90,000 hours at work over a lifetime.[1] For those who are unhappy or unsettled at work, it may seem longer. For those out of work, it can feel like a gaping hole. So, is our working life a result of a series of serendipitous circumstances? Or is it a question of perspective?

In this book, we're going to explore how nailing your narrative around your working life can be a fast track to discovering your own Hallmark ending—telling a story that's uniquely yours (maybe without the snow).

CHAPTER 2

WORK—THE LAST TABOO?

Here we'll explore the impact of career change in midlife and how the practice of narrative therapy can be adapted to apply to the workplace.

 **QUICK FIX**

- Inflationary economics, war, pandemics, mental health, sustainability and AI are all impacting how and when we work.

- Finding work in your middle age isn't easy—every second person in the world is believed to hold ageist attitudes.

- A holistic approach is needed to find employment or handle a job when you're in it—and resilience is a gamechanger.

- We all have a natural ability to tell stories that can help us be more resilient.

- Employing Narrative Practice can exploit the richness of our multi-storied working lives.

- This book shows how to apply the benefits of Narrative Practice to explore your goals, behaviours and attitudes and find new ways to be more ready and resilient in the workplace.

 to The role of the narrative

Find out more

Like many children growing up in the 1960s, pre-working life for my sister and me was simple. We did our best at school. We helped around the house. We behaved ourselves. With post-war parents who hadn't had the opportunity to finish their own education, there was also strong encouragement to go on to further education (in those days, with a grant that meant you wouldn't be bankrupted for life in the process). After that, we were told, the world was our oyster.

CHAPTER 2

It was simply a case of finding work and fitting in.

For many, the formula is similar today, except there is the added complication of a global outlook. Constant access to a world view makes inflationary economics, war, pandemics and the vagaries of mental health seem so much part of our personal back yard.

Employment trends come and go, but the expectation is that we will all be working well into later life and need to be increasingly flexible as the age of artificial intelligence (AI) replaces some existing roles altogether.

Fitting in at work has become less about an individual's approach and more about employers' promotable cultural fit as they declare their commitment to inclusion and diversity, sustainability and mental well-being.

As a freelance writer for nearly 30 years, I am well-versed in the peaks and troughs of supply and demand for work. An independent supplier can sit under the radar of office politics but is only as good as the last project. Work peaks can be exhilarating while the slower times serve to reignite the constant fear that you will never, ever, never work again.

Despite decades of this cycle—and a certain cosy familiarity with a major client's longstanding contract—in my '60s I was "let go" as a business writer with three days' notice in favour of AI writing software. Despite the hints of what was to come over the previous two years and witnessing a drip feed of brutal dismissals before that, I was still woefully unprepared for the sudden need to reappraise my motivations and my future.

A gamut of grief

Although I have subsequently suffered Kubler-Ross-style grief stages at "losing" my lifelong working pattern, I confess that my initial response was one of relief. Relief from the uncertainty of having the contract renewed a month at a time, generally on the last valid day and relief at no longer having to "play the game" in a corporate environment that could be called at best self-serving and at worst, toxic.

Of course, it wasn't all doom and gloom or just about the pay cheque—there were plenty of fair-minded and highly appreciative clients in the mix. But there were also moments when sheer willpower—and visualising my bank balance—was all that helped me get through the day.

Anyone who has worked for a large corporate organisation will recognise the gap that exists between corporate values and corporate behaviours. And sadly, in a business world that operates with a "sink or swim" mentality, many people either stay the course and find themselves struggling to keep their head above corporate culture waters or end up reaching for the lifejacket of a new role elsewhere.

EVERY SECOND PERSON IN THE WORLD IS BELIEVED TO HOLD AGEIST ATTITUDES.

Finding work later in life isn't easy. Even the World Health Organization has admitted ageism is a global challenge—with its report declaring that every second person in the world is believed to hold ageist attitudes.[2] The stigma of being expensive and less nimble is alive and well; it is ironic that experience is considered so irrelevant when you have it in spades later in life and so often requested at entry level jobs when the newly educated are struggling to get a foot in the door.

Who are you?

Do any of these statements sound familiar? Maybe it's time to take a closer look at your own narrative.

Looking for work…	Struggling in work …
"I'm 53 and I've just been made redundant for the third time in as many years."	"I don't think I can continue to work for a company that treats me like this."
"I've been out of work for four years now; after the pandemic, it's been hard to pick up where I left off."	"My boss has just been replaced by Cruella de Vil. I'm so unhappy."
"I don't feel well enough to work full-time—but I can't afford not to."	"Between my job, the kids and my parents, I feel like I'm failing all round."
"I've been out of the recruitment loop for so long, I'm really nervous about an interview—and don't even have a CV!"	"I'm nearly at retirement age but I'm worried about becoming an invisible pensioner."
"I keep applying for things but get nowhere. Most companies don't even reply."	"I can't keep pace with technology; I'm beginning to feel irrelevant and super stressed."

Not the right fit

When it comes to job search later in life, as our beloved Scottish bard would say "there's the rub"—looking for a job can serve as a reminder that you're too experienced or not experienced enough. You're lacking the right skills or you're overqualified. You're too dependent on a team or your independence and individuality infer that you're not a team player.

And while it can be hard to break in to an organisation, it can be equally easy to crash out from your current job when a difficult or demanding environment puts a strain on you over a long period of time, physically and mentally.

> **IN SOME WAYS, FINDING AND SECURING WORK IS ONE OF THE LAST TABOOS.**

It's often hard to admit being available or talk about the difficulties of being out of work. People have been criticised for adding the "open to work" badge on the popular business platform LinkedIn; while some argue it demonstrates positivity and accessibility, others suggest that the badge has a negative spin since "the best people aren't looking for work."

There's a certain stigma around multiple redundancies, even though these decisions are more often a lottery, rather than based on capabilities or personality. Constantly being told you are the runner up to getting the job can feel you're "always the bridesmaid, never the bride".

The process around finding work can be gruelling; instant rejection or no reply to a stream of applications can easily dampen even the most upbeat personality—especially when well-meaning friends suggest totally unsuitable career alternatives. There's absolutely nothing wrong with working for a high street retailer, but if you've been liaising with CEOs on digital transformation for the last 10 years, it's unlikely that it will feel like the next best career move.

CHAPTER 2

Before my contract ended, I started working with my local church, Upton Vale Baptist Church in Devon, on a course to help people (of all ages but many over 50) to get back into work. It has proved to be some of the most rewarding hours I've spent in my working lifetime.

Often lacking in confidence and without the fundamentals in place (such as having a CV) to secure a job, course participants attend a five-week programme that shares the tips and techniques to help them feel better prepared. I'm going to cover some of the aspects of the course later in the book, but from the outset I noticed that finding a job was just one of many challenges faced by course participants.

Some are in the throes of accommodation issues, have dependents or sick relatives, have limited access to the internet or technology options (no laptop or smart phone) or are bamboozled by the proliferation of digital technology options; all this they carry with them into the course—and it doesn't help as they try to negotiate a path to employment success.

It is clear that a more holistic approach is needed to address the task of finding employment—or handling a job when you're in it. And there is one qualification seldom mentioned that is an essential requirement whatever role is being sought—it's resilience.

With resilience on our side, any employment hurdles can be overcome, whether you're in or out of work. Yet, the role of resilience in the process of jobseeking is often underestimated.

 to Connecting with resilience

With all the qualifications or training in the world, unless you have the mindset and stamina to face rejection, disappointment, pressure and (sadly, sometimes) aggressive or biased cultures, then all your hopes and dreams for a successful working life are at risk.

In my personal view, resilience should be first and foremost on every employer's job specification and part of any school curriculum. A resilient mindset can not only help you gain the grit to stay the course, whatever difficulties you face, but also enable you to remain open and ready for that perfect opportunity that is just around the corner. We need to make resilience part of our career story.

OPEN. READY. RESILIENT.

You may be thinking "resilience, that old chestnut. I've read a million books on that already." And certainly, it's not a new topic. We can all learn about the steps we need to take or what resilience looks like. But what if there was something that comes quite naturally to us—and is part of our every day—that could bring those resilience efforts into sharper focus?

I'm referring to the role of the narrative; our personal narrative, what we tell ourselves and what we choose to share with others. The narrative is the thread that weaves life events together to form a story—and we all tell stories to make sense of our lives. Often without realising, we carry these narratives around with us; sometimes they are helpful and sometimes they are not. The story can become skewed, either by things we believe to be true or through events that have happened to us which direct us to make collective assumptions about what those events tell us.

Narrative Practice, sometimes referred to as narrative therapy, has been applied in the fields of psychotherapy and counselling since it was developed in the 1970s and 1980s. It stems from the intellectual partnership and friendship of family therapist **Michael White** and New Zealand therapist **David Epston** and is described by practitioner and author **Alice Morgan** as "a respectful, non-blaming approach to counselling and community work, which centres people as the experts in their own lives. It views problems as separate from people and assumes people have many skills, competencies, beliefs, values, commitments and abilities that will assist them to reduce the influence of problems in their lives."

I would argue the therapeutic environment isn't the only place where a better understanding of your narrative—and a reminder of your central expertise—could make a difference.

By exploring, deconstructing, and reconstructing your career narrative, you can gain new perspectives, challenge limiting beliefs and create more empowering stories.

THE NARRATIVE IS THE THREAD THAT WEAVES LIFE EVENTS TOGETHER TO FORM A STORY.

Whether seeking new work or re-evaluating a role, your personal narrative is a vital part of the process. During interviews, employers look for those individual stories that bring your experience to life. Whether you are in or out of work, being clear (and honest) about your personal narrative could make all the difference to fulfilling and rewarding work experiences—and help you to live a more authentic life.

Since the pandemic, our personal and professional lives have merged, faster and with greater intensity than ever before due to the ease and availability of digital experiences. Our smartphones are no longer simply a communications tool—they offer access to our work emails while running our social diary, document our experiences through endless photo capture or showcase our talents through podcasts, video diaries or Instagram.

Since our personal and professional lives are blending like never before, it's time to embrace some of the practices that separated those lives in the past. For this reason, I believe it makes sense to introduce psychotherapy or counselling techniques, specifically Narrative Practice, to harmonise our everyday employment demands.

NARRATIVE PRACTICE CAN BE GOOD FOR OUR PERSONAL WELL-BEING AND GOOD FOR BUSINESS.

This book takes a deeper dive into some of the fundamental practicalities that can build and maintain resilience. We'll explore some of the tools of Narrative Practice and how they can be applied in your own life today to grow that resilience.

Along the way, we'll be tiptoeing around influencing factors such as the brain's neuroplasticity[3] and the role of the vagal nerve—the mind-body balance.

 to Resilience fundamentals/A need to understand your own behaviours

I'll also be drawing on a plethora of stories and ideas from others and offering some takeaways to ease your own resilience journey.

FEEL STRONGER, BE BRAVER AND SHARE YOUR AUTHENTIC SELF.

Through these pages I hope we can all begin to abandon the taboos of midlife and unemployment, especially when those two elements happen to coincide.

If you have been experiencing difficult times, I can assure you, you are not alone. I encourage you to read that again with feeling—you are NOT alone.

As a midlifer, you will already have seen many things, but nothing can prepare you for the feelings of hopelessness in the face of constant rejection. Equally, experience isn't always helpful at work when your team, boss or HR department fails to act with integrity or consider your well-being.

Change needn't mean loss. Although it can be irritating to hear "when one door closes, another opens" during times of unplanned change, the fact is you can't make space for new or better experiences if you are constantly consumed by work or life distractions.

FIND A NEW WAY TO BE MORE READY AND RESILIENT IN THE WORKPLACE.

By examining the factors that contribute to readiness and resilience—whether in the workplace or during a job search—you can start to align your values, personality, talents and aspirations in ways that feel authentic and recognised.

Taking the time to reflect on the stories that have shaped your journey so far, and reframing them through the lens of resilience, enables midlife career frustrations to evolve into opportunities for personal and professional growth. With a focus on nailing your narrative you can redefine not only how you see yourself but also how others perceive you. Let's take a closer look at midlife's muddles and motivations.

CHAPTER 3

MIDLIFE MAYHEM

Midlife can seem chaotic. Career paths feel stagnant, family dynamics change, and existing views about work and success may no longer fit. In this chapter we'll examine how to better manage midlife.

QUICK FIX

- Being out of work in midlife can be a shock and prompt a range of emotions.
- Surveys show a rise in "no-response applications" and the increased use of AI to filter candidates.
- Midlifers can find their narrative influenced by many factors: education, emotional intelligence, workplace culture, workforce dynamics, baggage, health and family.
- Consider new ways to rethink an unhelpful story you may be telling yourself today.

 **to Managing midlife**

 WORKBOOK TIP:
Exercise 3.3 Reauthor your life.

Find out more

The older I get, the more I stretch the term midlifer. While it's typically associated with people in their 40s and 50s, 60 can feel like the new 40—especially for those who had children later in life, are adjusting their work patterns to care for ageing parents or are continuing their careers out of financial necessity. It may also be a lonely time for empty nesters who are looking to keep working to maintain relationships that matter or forge new friendships.

You've no doubt heard it said that age is all in the mind and, in truth, if your health is intact, those bigger number birthdays do tend to slip by unnoticed. Then one day you find yourself working on a project being supervised by someone young enough to be your child or the latest wave of redundancies hits and you find yourself on the "experienced and expensive" pile.

FIVE STAGES OF GRIEF—DENIAL, ANGER, BARGAINING, DEPRESSION, ACCEPTANCE.

As I mentioned earlier, being laid off later in life can result in a range of different emotions. Kubler-Ross talked about five stages of grief—denial, anger, bargaining, depression and acceptance—and it is possible to feel some or all these stages of grief if you are asked to leave a responsible job with a steady income.

Even if you planned on retirement, the switch from being busy and under pressure (something you thought you wanted to shake off for years) can be a shock. Moving from managing a team of people or "always on" working to suit your global company's time zones, to wondering if it's time to take the dog for a walk or pick up the groceries, can be a difficult transition.

Loss of the identifiable status of employment can be hard in other ways, too. Meeting anyone for the first time will generally result in the question: "And what do you do?" while family and friends may suddenly feel you are in a position to offer them unlimited time to fix things, ferry them around or listen to a range of their latest suggestions on what you can do with your time.

Whether you have been made redundant or have had difficulty finding employment for some time, it is understandable to feel anger or resentment. No one likes to feel invisible, and it can often seem as if the cards are stacked against you when there are high volumes of people applying for the same job. It appears to be a general trend now to ignore applications if they are deemed unsuitable.

Failing to send even a one-line response to those who don't qualify for interview or are simply not in the running is quite rude. It only needs a sentence such as: "Thank you for your interest but we will not be pursuing your application at this time" to acknowledge that someone has taken the time and effort to show interest in your organisation—and leaves a far better impression of the calibre and culture within the company by doing so.

According to an article in *The Sunday Times*,[4] recent university leavers describe the process of job hunting as "frustrating" and "disheartening". They say they are "burnt out" after dedicating many hours to job applications only to be "ghosted" by employers. The article reflects how AI is playing a role, too.

In an IBM survey of more than 8,500 global IT professionals showed 42% of companies in 2023 used AI screening "to improve recruiting and human resources," while another 40% of respondents were considering integrating the technology. And there is a danger, as companies are increasingly relying on intelligence-driven hiring platforms, that some of the human interaction that lies at the heart of good relationships at work will be lost.

People often say hindsight is a wonderful thing and, as a midlifer, there is a lot to be said for having "been there, seen that, bought the tee-shirt." But along with that experience and knowledge can come a history of regret about choices and decision making and difficulty in accepting the "new you" as you grapple with changes to your appearance and lifestyle.

Social media with its avenue to the past and the present can highlight comparisons with schoolfriends or work colleagues that is less than helpful. If you're unemployed, it's unlikely you will want to be reminded of your friend living the dream with that geeky guy she met at school who now owns a multi-million-dollar tech company. Or see the photos of the former boss sunning herself in St Lucia, toenails perfectly painted and a pina colada in hand.

Midlife can also bring its fair share of illness, financial issues, marital discord, or family deaths—and yes, the mad mess that is the menopause which can affect women, men and employers. For the ladies that have never experienced a hot flush during a conference call with a bunch of middle-aged men, consider yourself lucky.

Against the backdrop of these challenges, focusing on the next opportunity can be demoralising and draining, often taking a toll on personal confidence.

Let's delve deeper into the key issues that arise when you're either seeking new work or feeling dissatisfied in your current role, exploring the elements and actions within these scenarios.

Managing midlife

Here are some of the elements that influence your narrative as a jobseeker or employee:

1. Education is seen to be the cornerstone of our future working lives. And yet every school's curriculum is focused on academic achievement and rarely features preparation for work environments—or the sheer tenacity needed to find work for the rest of your life.

If you've followed a particular path up to now but want to switch professions to broaden your job prospects, undertaking courses or enhancing qualifications can be a good way to boost your profile and your confidence. In an era of Massive Open Online Courses (MOOCs)[5], this additional learning need not come with the price tag of standard postgraduate educational avenues either and can fill in the blanks on some of the life skills elements of education. In the UK, the Government runs free courses on its Skills for Careers website[6] and, of course, local libraries are a good source of information for learning and development.

Understandably, self-learning requires motivation which can be in short supply if you are out of work for a long time, don't enjoy studying, or feel that is part of your past academic life.

2. Emotional intelligence. Like most pursuits, there is an art to getting work—and keeping it. Minimum qualifications are important, of course, to maintain standards to meet a role's skillset and demands. But strength of character and applying emotional intelligence in a working context are equally relevant skills.

A report from CapGemini found that 74% of executives believe emotional intelligence is set to be a "must have" skill in the next five years with returns on their investment in building emotional intelligence in their workforces potentially offering incremental gains of US$6.8 million.[7] And with some studies suggesting that older adults may use their increased emotional intelligence to enhance their subjective well-being,[8] that's a serious vote in favour of educating ourselves in how we are as well as why we are at work.

> **74% OF EXECUTIVES BELIEVE EMOTIONAL INTELLIGENCE WILL BECOME A "MUST-HAVE" SKILL FOR ALL EMPLOYEES IN THE NEXT FIVE YEARS.[9]**

3. Workplace culture. There's general consensus that workplaces and workforces have changed. Post-COVID-19, the era of home working has well and truly arrived with many companies struggling to insist on an office-based presence if they want to retain the best staff. The shift has implications for work culture, productivity and work-life balance.

According to working from home (WFH) statistics compiled on the website The Home Office Life[10] in the United Kingdom, between 2020 and 2024 from various source reports, 58% of workers prefer to work in a hybrid model and 52% of business leaders surveyed believe that hybrid working is the most supportive environment for employee productivity. But there are suggestions of a generational divide—81% of younger workers said they would feel more isolated without time in the office.[11]

4. Workforce dynamics have changed, partly due to office presence and partly due to changes from the digital age. Social media has steered us toward the power of the individual voice—the rise of influencers, the ability to make or break a brand through negative feedback or new opportunities to showcase talent, products or services.

In a noisy "look at me" world, authoritarian and hierarchical workforce structures are a poor fit. Democratic freedom is a luxury we all deserve, but the absence of a code of conduct can be a slippery slope. Have you worked in a place where some people clearly don't know how to behave?

Actions and attitudes such as talking over others in meetings (think: politicians during an election debate), a lack of common courtesies, or being offensive in front of customers can stir unrest and division that negates any company culture—no matter how many times the company's values proclaim that its employees act with integrity and respect.

5. Baggage. It would be hard to get to midlife without finding you're travelling along life's road with a certain number of ready-baked opinions or ideas. True, some of these experiences are helpful (knowing when not to leave things to the last minute or your intuition about the new person who's just joined the accounts team can be useful in fending off difficult or demanding situations). But relying on these well-worn experiences can also work against us.

We often hold a certain amount of unconscious bias and occasionally this can spill over unhelpfully into person-to-person situations at work. For instance, in the aviation industry, some female pilots' competence has been called into question from passengers (or male colleagues[12]) simply on the basis of gender.[13] Or we may find that bias becomes a sticking point at an interview if the interviewer reminds you of someone you know with unpleasant characteristics or attitude. Baggage is easy to acquire and hard to shift.

6. Health matters are a strong influencer when it comes to personal capabilities. Perhaps you have experienced ongoing mental health issues or survived cancer; these conditions can change how we see the world and lead to a layer of self-preservation which can be both helpful and limiting.

In my early 30s, I was hospitalised with glandular fever; it is a condition that affects the immune system and, much like COVID-19, can be hard to shake off. For me, the debilitating tiredness lasted around a year and left me with a legacy of concern about "overdoing things" that made me hesitate from embracing too active a social life—for many years I made a choice to work rather than play because I knew I was unlikely to have the stamina to do both.

But in the words of the old proverb: "All work and no play makes Jack a dull boy", it's important to look after your health by balancing the time you spend at work and your personal time, at play with hobbies, people and pastimes you enjoy. Indeed, play—including digital gaming—can help us to rewire our brains and redesign our future. It has been shown that the gaming experience helps people collaborate, co-create, and embrace a new way of thinking.[14] Look at your health as a whole and listen to what your body needs.

PLAY IS AN IMPORTANT PART OF REDESIGNING OUR FUTURE.

7. Family commitments are another major influence on who you are and how you present yourself to the world. In particular, later in life women often wear multiple hats—mother, daughter, wife, bestie, agony aunt, often in that order—and these factors affect our working lives.

Gender gap ageism

In its long-time series gender pay gap report, the Office for National Statistics[15] notes:

⬆ **10.3%** the gender pay gap for full-time employees aged 40 to 49 years and older.

⬆ **4.7%** the pay gap doubled among employees aged 30 to 39 years between 2022 and 2023.

⬆ **14.2%** the gender pay gap for full-time employees aged 60 years and over increased from 13.5% to 14.2% between 2022 and 2023, the largest gap of all age groups.

It's also worth noting that ageism isn't just affecting older workers, especially if you're female. In McKinsey's tenth Women in the Workplace research,[16] in partnership with LeanIn.Org, the largest study of women in corporate America, women remain underrepresented at every stage of the corporate pipeline and continue to face barriers.

At the beginning of their careers, women are far less likely than men to attain their very first promotion to a manager role—a situation that's not improving. About half of women under 30 say their age played a role in missing out on opportunities at work; they are almost twice as likely as younger men to field unwanted comments about their age.

According to a March report published by the UK government[17] there were 10.05 million women working full time in October to December 2023, while 6.01 million were working part-time. To juggle their many commitments, women constitute the lion's share of part-time working—38% of all women in employment worked part-time, compared with 14% of men.

Pay equity is still an issue: Median weekly pay for female full-time employees was £629 in April 2023, according to data from the ONS Annual Survey of Hours and Earnings. This compared with £725 for male full-time employees. It's easy to see how your personal story can drift when viewing these statistics.

And, of course, it's not just a female issue. Many men are still wearing their breadwinner status as a badge of honour, so it can be doubly hard to accept that they are the dependent, for however short a period, or that they cannot provide for their family.

HUMILIATION ~~STINKS~~ STICKS

In my university placement year, I worked at a construction and leisure company in the centre of Bristol. The work was straightforward and structured but seeing corporate working life "up close and personal" for the first time at 19 years old was an unexpected education.

I was shocked at how many people seemed to be hiding their true feelings about their work and the company behind a veneer of business duty and discipline. On my last day, the boss, who had barely acknowledged me up to that point, asked me what I thought of the company. In my naivety, I told him I was disappointed that not many people seemed to really enjoy their jobs (I hear you, not my finest hour for diplomacy).

His response was to march me out into the main working area and physically push me in the back from one desk to the next demanding of his employees: "Sarah doesn't think you're very happy here. Do you enjoy your job?" Everyone reassured him that everything was fine. I can still vividly remember the fear in their eyes and my own humiliation 40 years on.

Of course, this is my telling of the story—let's say, to use an ugly but popular phrase, it's "my truth". But as our wise, wonderful and deeply missed Queen Elizabeth II said: "some recollections may vary".

What if I told you that story another way?

HERE'S A RE-WRITE—SPOT THE DIFFERENCES.

In my university placement year, I worked at a construction and leisure company in the centre of Bristol. The work helped me to understand how a business runs and, for a naïve 19-year-old, it was an education in more ways than one. I got to know the staff and to me they didn't seem to be very happy in their work.

On my last day the busy CEO asked me about my placement. I told him I was disappointed that not many people seemed to really enjoy their jobs. He took me into the open plan office and said to each of his employees: "Sarah doesn't think you're very happy here. Do you enjoy your job?" Everyone reassured him that they were fine.

I have felt rewarded ever since that I discovered, so early in my career, that there is a time and place to reveal our authentic selves. It was also a swift education about the importance of company culture. These two learnings prepared me well for corporate life and helped me gain the stamina and sensitivity to maintain a 30-year freelance career.

Better? Does this shift your understanding of the event from "an early insight into corporate shaming and game playing—and a tough lesson in opinion sharing"—to "a valuable lesson in office life, human nature and a positive steer towards a career as an independent consultant"?

Obviously, using a different turn of phrase and vocabulary can make all the difference to our interpretation of events—you only need to read a few different headlines in the daily papers to see how a story can be twisted to develop an entirely different meaning.

But there is a deeper shift here between the two versions of the story: in the first, I hang on to that humiliation and fear, making it part of my own career "failings". In the second, I put that incident down to experience, learning to channel the emotional response into an incentive that opens the door to future opportunities and personal growth.

It is this kind of nuanced narrative that can be helpful to understand as you take your next steps. I'm not suggesting you deny difficult circumstances in your life. But reframing experiences lies at the heart of Narrative Practice, and we'll look a little deeper at how we can repurpose a negative experience or memory, effectively and authentically, and transform it to your benefit.

TRY NOW: Do you have career a story from the past where you felt humiliated, upset or disappointed? Consider rewriting that story in the manner of the example here, using different words to soften your interpretation of the event and allow yourself to see the potential for positive outcomes from your experience.

 WORKBOOK TIP:
Exercise 3.3 Reauthor your life.

CHAPTER 4

WHAT MIDLIFE **JOBSEEKERS** SHOULD KNOW

Unemployed and unhappy—is this you?

Whether you've been out of work for a while or recently "let go", it's rarely welcome news to be unemployed. The period in between career moves can be isolating and disheartening.

Let's take a deeper dive into the fundamentals for midlife jobseekers to secure their next best position and hear how some people have changed their story and their work prospects.

 WORKBOOK TIP: Take a look at Section 1 BEING READY for exercises that explore this topic further.

 **QUICK FIX**

- Being out of work in midlife is not your first rodeo—persistence will pay off.

- Jobseekers need to reframe rejection, welcome the art of the possible and recognise that the era of AI requires us to be more human, exploiting our unique qualities of ideation, innovation and intuition.

- Neuroplasticity (rewiring our brains) helps us to not only connect with resilience but also adapt to reorganise our thoughts and behaviours.

- Move toward emotional intelligence and away from underestimating our potential; be clear about who you are.

- Read about 2B Ready, a course that is helping jobseekers to be ready and resilient for work and the stories of successful 2BR participants.

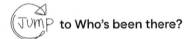 to Who's been there?

Find out more

When you find yourself out of work in midlife, it's helpful to remember this is not your first rodeo—you've experienced this situation before, perhaps a few times in your career, and you know that persistence will pay off. But there's nothing like the here and now to make you feel that this time it's different.

Indeed, you may have some additional factors creep in as we've seen—concerns over ageism, keeping up with technological progress (especially the variety of ways to communicate and participate) and being pulled in many different directions through demands of family or personal health and well-being concerns.

While "bad" experiences can be as helpful as good ones in shaping us, there are a few elements that can influence our jobseeking journey:

The need to reframe rejection: No experience is ever wasted—predicting how things might turn out or making assumptions about a situation can be highly inaccurate and disruptive in the long run.

Every time we say: "I'll never be any good at [insert skill or capability here]" we're negatively influencing ourselves as well as others and shaping a narrative that is hard to shift.

Embrace your own potential and that of others.

 WORKBOOK TIP: Exercise 2.4 Explore the Tree of Life

Collaborative practices can be fruitful and rewarding. In one of his last interviews, the late author and poet **John O'Donohue** talked about his work with large corporations. He said when someone is doing their dream job it's an expression of their gift—but the gift is not meant for them alone.

Sharing skills and talents should be for the benefit of communities and leadership should encourage an environment where they are able to thrive. Competitive corporate environments that focus on self-congratulation and one-upmanship often fail to take advantage of the benefits of these collaborative practices, perhaps to their detriment.

 **to Locked loneliness**

Welcome the art of the possible: Popular in British reality television, the fallacy "you can be anything you want" has seen at least two generations where this idea has been actively encouraged. That's not to say it isn't worth striving for what you want or setting goals, but even "The X-Factor" and "Britain's Got Talent" entrepreneur **Simon Cowell** would have to admit that being a world-class basketball player at his age and with his health history is somewhat out of reach.

And in some instances, we may be following a path we think is right at the cost of the one that is. **Vera Wang** may have taken the fashion world by storm, but she didn't start out with that career in mind. A viral sensation at the age of 72, she pursued a career as a figure skater but after 16 years she had to accept that it was not working out.

Following her interest in the fashion industry, she worked for prestigious publications such as *Vogue* before launching her own bridal boutique. In an exclusive BBC 100 Women interview[18] she shared how she was able to use all the skills from that earlier career path to not only ease, but also influence and augment this career transition.

What unexpected role might you take in the future?

 WORKBOOK TIP: Exercise 3.1 Throw away the rule book

The AI era forces us to be "more human": Shifts in AI technologies mean that many of us are finding new ways to live and work. ChatGPT, a chatbot that enables users to refine and steer a conversation towards a desired length, format, style, level of detail and language used, reached 100 million monthly active users just two months after it launched, making it the fastest-growing consumer application in history.

CHAPTER 4

 to How to get started

Every week there is a new media story about the impact of robotics and automation on jobs—whether that's through the speed and scale of analytics processing or the physical infallibility that enables robots to sustain challenging work practices, such as working in sewer systems or aiding patients needing healthcare.

An MIT Technology Review article reported an interview in 2023 between the UK prime minister at the time, Rishi Sunak, and Elon Musk where the latter declared there will come a time when "no job is needed," thanks to an AI "magic genie that can do everything you want".[19]

Indeed, in a survey on the future of jobs by the World Economic Forum[20] (which describes itself as an international organisation for public-private cooperation), employers estimated that 44% of workers' skills will be disrupted in the next five years. It suggests that artificial intelligence is expected to be adopted by nearly 75% of surveyed companies and is expected to lead to high churn—with 50% of organisations expecting it to create job growth and 25% expecting it to create job losses.

Yet, while machines may replace humans in some jobs, there is an opportunity for humans to excel at the skills where AI is currently less reliable. Ideation, innovation and intuition are human qualities which machine learning currently struggles to emulate, making a case for the power of individuality and reassuring the doomsayers that the work of human beings is heading for extinction.

 to Future-proof resilience

Connecting with resilience

The concept of being authors of our own lives is not a new one; 25 years ago, American psychologist and philosopher **Eugene Gendlin** stated that the ability to connect with our inner lives, our feelings and intuition, was vital to our overall well-being.[21]

In a process he called focusing, he recommends awareness of your "felt sense", the body's sense of a particular problem or situation, and suggests that by certain steps this felt sense can come into focus. This body shift gets to the crux of life's problems so that they seem different—in short, we create change ourselves, from within.

For the control freaks among you, the idea that we can "heal ourselves" is an attractive one. For others, you may be feeling (to commandeer a familiar saying) …

SOME ARE BORN RESILIENT,

SOME ACHIEVE RESILIENCE,

SOME HAVE RESILIENCE THRUST UPON THEM.

Yet, the idea that we are resilient or not is just an illusion. Neuroscientists reliably inform us that we are all capable of neuroplasticity—that is, an ability to rewire our brains (Figure 1).

Recent studies[22] have shown we can still develop new neural pathways even later in life by undertaking such tasks as learning a new language or a musical instrument. Case studies of stroke victims show that the brain can use other, non-damaged areas of the brain to pick up the functionality that the damaged areas are no longer able to serve.[23]

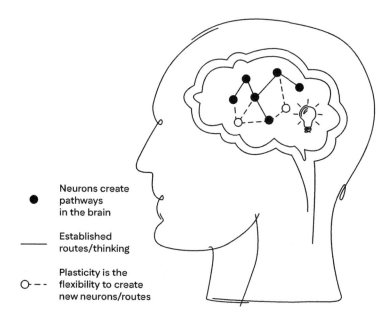

Figure 1. Neuroplasticity means we can all rewire our brains.

This ability to adapt means that the power to become resilient, even if you have crippling anxiety or fear, is available to you. Think about that for a moment.

Powerful progress

Alongside letting our body solve our challenges, it's a powerful idea that we have an ability to change and adapt and reorganise our thoughts and behaviours. There's an interesting book by a Canadian author and lecturer **Barbara Arrowsmith-Young** about rewiring our brains to think differently or tackle tasks differently.

She was born with severe learning disabilities that hampered her education and caused the teachers to label her as slow and stubborn. Indeed, she was once given the strap (many years before health and safety rules!) in front of the whole class as the teacher thought she was being disobedient.

As a child, she read and wrote everything backwards, was physically uncoordinated and she continually got lost. But through sheer willpower she made her way to graduate school where she found research that inspired her to invent cognitive exercises to "fix" her own brain.

In her book "The Woman Who Changed Her Brain" Arrowsmith-Young tells her personal story with case histories from 30 years of working with children and adults. She was also featured in an Amazon Prime video with Dr Norman Doidge on "The Brain that Changes Itself"[24] which showed Arrowsmith-Young now leading a programme to educate students with similar issues to herself.

Rewiring our brains depends on more than an understanding of brain mechanics. Even long before the revelations from brain studies, a Viennese psychiatrist and Holocaust survivor, **Viktor E. Frankl**, recognised the importance of our attitude and thinking when faced with difficulties.

During and partly because of his suffering, he developed a new therapy, known as logotherapy, based on the belief that human nature is motivated by the search for a life purpose. His books "Man's Search for Meaning" and "The Unheard Cry for Meaning" talk about the unique human potential to transform a tragedy into a personal triumph and to turn difficulties into achievements. He says:

> "WHEN WE ARE NO LONGER ABLE TO CHANGE A SITUATION, WE ARE CHALLENGED TO CHANGE OURSELVES".

Helping people to be ready

I've been reminded of this need for resilience at a personal level following the charitable work I mentioned earlier. Upton Vale Baptist Church had looked at what was needed to help our community and recognised that employment, or the lack of it, was a significant issue among the local populus. It licensed a third-party's packaged programme to get people aged 18+ into work and recruited suitable participants. I began volunteering with this programme to assist in coaching jobseekers.

Not long after my involvement, the third-party course coordinators decided to discontinue the course. At this stage, with the need established, I was asked to write a new course—and was delighted to have an opportunity to embrace a holistic approach to training jobseekers, one that puts resilience front and centre.

Although the jobseekers' fundamentals of having a CV or documented work history and good interview technique is important, we focus the course content on building confidence and grit, so that participants can more easily ride the waves of difficulties and obstacles that hamper their jobseeking efforts.

Redundancy and job application rejection make it easy to follow the well-worn path of thinking we are not good enough—or gradually erode any confidence that we were. But there are many avenues that can offer encouragement to revise the stories that we tell ourselves.

Particularly relevant for midlife jobseekers is the work of **Daniel Goleman** who authored the groundbreaking book on "Emotional intelligence".[25] In it, he talks about the fact that IQ is not nearly as much our destiny as we think. He says our emotions play a far greater role in thought, decision making and individual success and managing our own career needs us to recognise "our deepest feelings about what we do—and what changes might make us more truly satisfied with our work."

Goleman isn't suggesting we all burst into tears when things don't go our way, but he is explaining that those people who are in tune with their own emotions, take responsibility for them and are sensitive to the needs of others can be more successful, personally and professionally.

Interestingly, it is Goleman who also refuted the idea proposed by **Malcolm Gladwell** around the 10,000-hour rule—the idea that this is the amount of time one must invest in practice to reach meaningful success in any field. Goleman states that the secret to continued improvement isn't the *amount* of time invested but the *quality* of that time[26]—and for midlifers, the quality argument is pertinent if they are shifting careers.

Similarly, you can take heart from the findings of **Adam Grant** in his book "Hidden Potential"[27] that makes a case for anyone being able to rise to achieve greater things. The author says: "the true measure of your potential is not the height of the peak you've reached, but how far you've climbed to get there".

In the book, he tells a heartwarming story about the National Junior High Chess Championships in Detroit. The tournament was usually won by teams from private schools where chess was part of the curriculum. A team called the Raging Rooks consisted of poor students who lived in neighbourhoods rife with drugs, violence and crime decided to enter the tournament. Some of them had only just learned the game of chess. One of them practiced in a park with a drug dealer. And yet they beat the reigning champions and went on to achieve bigger and better things.

The author suggests the differences in a successful life is not so much down to natural ability, but our responses to opportunity and motivation. Even more powerful in this story is that their coach, Maurice Ashley, saw the potential in them that neither they nor their parents saw in themselves. He concludes that we don't just underestimate ourselves; sometimes the people who know us best underestimate us, too.[28]

SUCCESS IS DOWN TO OUR RESPONSE TO OPPORTUNITY AND MOTIVATION.

Another author who tackles the issues head on that relate to resilience is research professor **Brené Brown**. Her commentary on courage, vulnerability, shame and empathy has seen her challenge some of the big taboos around these topics and ease our understanding of ourselves.

In "Braving the Wilderness: The Quest for True Belonging and the Courage to Stand Alone"[29] Brown reflects on the role of belonging in an increasingly divisive and disconnected world. Her research examined how people feel and their concerns around belonging—and her findings are especially relevant if you are heading for a corporate culture whose values are misaligned with your own. She believes belonging is a practice that prompts us to be vulnerable and uncomfortable so that we can learn how to be present without sacrificing who we are.

Being who we are helps us maintain or build connections—giving us the resilience to navigate difficult conversations or circumstances—by understanding each other's motives and interests more closely. Brown says:

"TRUE BELONGING DOESN'T REQUIRE US TO CHANGE WHO WE ARE; IT REQUIRES US TO **BE** WHO WE ARE".

In midlife, the time is ripe to find the confidence to say: "this is me, warts and all".

Resilience fundamentals

So, how can resilience be baked into the job search process? One powerful example is the 2B Ready programme, developed in Devon.

Designed as a series of two-hour sessions over five weeks, the course illustrates how structure and support can transform the jobseeking experience. It uses the mnemonic READY to guide participants through practical advice, hands-on exercises and coaching support, creating a framework that helps jobseekers feel more prepared and confident in navigating the world of work (see Figure 2).

	RESEARCH	Be prepared	How can you be more ready for work?
	EXCELLENCE	Be better	What are the qualities you most admire in yourself and others?
	ACTION	Be active	What else can you do to serve your goals?
	DANGERS, OPPORTUNITIES, STRENGTHS	Be aware	How can you bring your best self to every interview?
	YOU	Be yourself	What will you take away for the future?

Figure 2. 2B Ready course content structure. Visit www.2bready.co.uk for more.

The accent is on getting the fundamentals right; for instance, it's important to have a current summary of the full extent of your skills and experience. A CV is still one of the best ways to do this, but best practice is to limit the content to two pages. This can be challenging for the midlifer who has often worked in many different environments and may want to add the finer details of them all.

It can be helpful to consider the "red thread" that connects different areas of your experience—for example, the five years spent as a quality consultant in a manufacturing plant show an eye for thoroughness and detail that will be helpful in seeking employment in a tightly regulated industry like finance. A previous role managing a supply chain could be useful experience in a retail business that needs to liaise with an ecosystem of suppliers. You may not have considered it, but often your experience builds a pattern that can be helpful later in life or as a step along the way to pursue your "North Star" career choice.

It often takes three or four weeks for us to see the full potential from jobseekers' CVs; they may have simply forgotten previous successes or not realised that the work was relevant. As a result, we work on CVs from day one, discussing and fine tuning to tease out every useful nugget.

Even "spare time" activities can be a good indicator of employability—those three years volunteering at the local dog rescue home show a kind and caring nature and a commitment that bodes well for a career in healthcare or a veterinary practice, even if your working life has been spent in retail.

One of the other areas that runs through many of the sessions is preparation for the interview process. Although it's possible to feel euphoric when an interview goes well, there are few of us who would claim to "enjoy" interviews. Whichever way you look at it, it feels like you're on trial; it's easy to be so focused on the points you want to get across or so nervous that you fail to pay attention to the question being asked, talk too much or share too little in your responses.

Locked loneliness

There is always the sense that large corporations place considerable effort and interest in establishing and maintaining corporate cultures. But such organisations can often make your working experience alienating and inhospitable—your daily grind can end up, to steal a phrase from George Orwell's 1984, as "the locked loneliness in which one had to live".

There may be annual employee surveys, carefully curated and shared with reassurances that changes will be made. The organisation might put itself forward and achieve significant presence in industry rankings— scoring well on the best company to work for, top 50 diversity company or most admired company listings. And yet day-to-day these accolades do not reflect the reality for its employees.

In truth, there is probably only one person that really matters—the CEO. In any job search it's worth trying to understand the nature, background and personal profile of the CEO as the approach of that person has a ripple effect throughout the organisation. In smaller companies, this person is the figurehead that everyone sees. In larger organisations, the ethos and approach of that person is often replicated by the executives in the next level(s) down.

It's worth finding out about the CEO's political allegiances, what company they keep socially, how former direct reports speak about their experiences with the CEO. It's worth knowing, too, what measures the C-suite has put in place for how the company treats its suppliers—if they're seen as easily replaceable, it hints at the CEO's personal integrity and commitment.

There's nothing more dissatisfying than feeling like you are a square peg in a round hole when it comes to corporate culture, so pay attention to how these values and attitudes add up. Make sure you do your homework (use platforms such as Glassdoor and Trustpilot) to look beyond how the company portrays itself. See how the company compares with other companies in the same or similar industry, so your assessment is on a level playing field.

ARE YOU CLEVER/SMART/INTERESTING ENOUGH TO BEAT 500+ CANDIDATES?

While you may be up against some fierce competition for your next role, you can always be the best you can be. Spend time looking at the influence of body language. In the simplified version of Professor Albert Mehrabian's[30] findings around understanding non-verbal communications:

- 7% of meaning in the words that are spoken.

- 38% of meaning is paralinguistic (the way that the words are said).

- 55% of meaning in facial expression.

It's quite staggering to think that our body language communicates more than half of what we say. That's not to say that words don't matter, but just that there are a lot of other clues to who you are, your state of mind or relationship to the person you're talking to and we're all processing these clues all the time, often without realising.

You know that moment when meeting someone for the first time where you have an instant understanding? Either knowing that you're going to get along or an instant dislike, without a logical reason why. The person in question may not even have spoken to us at all; there's just something about their demeanour, presence or aura, call it what you like, that seems to give us clarity about how we feel about them.

Here's a resilience checklist to aid those who are struggling to find employment or wondering how to move forward from setbacks. The checklist is a refresher of all the topics covered on the course and written simply to appeal to those who might want to keep themselves on track every day:

1. **Be well prepared**: research all opportunities and be clear and positive about what you're looking for.

2. **Aim to be the best you can**: know what excellence looks like for you and how you can set your mind to achieve it.

3. **Keep moving forward**: take action, even if you're unsure if it's the "right step," to change the dynamic and outcomes.

4. **Be confident in your strengths**: "trial run" your interviews and prepare your personal stories.

5. **Look after yourself**: be ready to step out of your comfort zone and be open to possibilities.

Who's been there?

> "What would life be if we had no courage to attempt anything?"
>
> Vincent Van Gogh

Seeing the effects of changes in personal confidence and resilience can be astonishing. Take the case of **Michael**[31], out of work in his 60s, whose first words on joining the 2B Ready course were: "I've done loads of these courses, they're never any good". He then proceeded to criticise all the other participants who he had met at the recruitment sign-up meeting.

CHAPTER 4

Through the subsequent weeks, we discovered Michael had been battling severe Type 1 diabetes for many years which disturbed his sleep and affected his movement. He was also having difficulty with some features on his mobile phone.

Following some phone instruction, a further visit to the nurse to improve his diabetes monitoring, additions to his CV that better illustrated the scope of his skills, and a "lightbulb moment" proposal that he worked part-time to better manage his health, Michael's whole approach transformed.

On the last day, he left the course saying: "I know what to do now. I'm going to recommend this course to others."

Similarly, **Rosemary** in her 40s who came to us without any formal employment history. Her background included having suffered abuse and neglect as a child and alcohol and mental health issues later in life that had forced her to become reclusive and detached from society.

She started the course highly nervous about her own situation and lack of job experience and told us she felt overwhelmed and fearful. But after the five-weeks of coaching and encouragement she told us she'd learned a lot and felt more confident about identifying her personal strengths, how to apply for jobs and do interviews.

Most of all, she was proud that she now had a CV that she could use going forward, detailing her various voluntary roles—something she thought she could never have with her limited experience of the job market.

Martha came to the 2B Ready course having been recently made redundant from a local design company. She had just turned 66 and was apprehensive about the future, especially since she could not afford to retire.

While Martha had many transferable skills, a background of an abusive relationship meant she suffered from low self-esteem and occasional lapses in concentration. Through careful guidance and instruction, she commented how the course was both efficient and impactful and had helped her with her confidence.

She felt the relaxed atmosphere "builds people up with possibilities and new ways to see your future". At this stage in her life, she was grateful for the opportunity to be with like-minded people who understood her challenges.

It is not easy on a page to convey the emotional uplift experienced by these participants through some dedicated instruction and effort. There's real joy, too, from being privileged enough to see that awakening within themselves. In short, achieving resilience—or at least experiencing the building blocks—is extremely gratifying for everyone involved.

The 2B Ready course is practical introduction to readiness and resilience at work. And changing your narrative can influence that jobseeking journey.

 to The role of the narrative

 TRY NOW: Use your home office or a space where you feel safe to set yourself regular reminders of what matters and where you are headed. Write yourself words of encouragement or identify goals on sticky notes and place them in strategic places around the room. Allow yourself to read them daily, even when they are familiar to you.

 WORKBOOK TIP:
Exercise 3.4 Revisit reminders.

A WORD ABOUT EMOTIONS

Oprah Winfrey is an American talk show host, television producer, actress and author. She is probably best known for The Oprah Winfrey Show, a talk show which ran for 25 years. Yet, her journalistic career didn't start well.

In the late 1970s, Winfrey was working as a news anchor and reporter at Baltimore's WJZ station—and the feedback from her bosses was far from positive. As she shared with CNBC[32]: "They told me I was the wrong colour, the wrong size, and that I showed too much emotion". In time, of course, she proved them wrong.

Much has been written over the years about leaving our emotions behind at work, so that we make clear-minded informed decisions. Emotions are part of our human experience. If we are to be our authentic selves, we need to employ emotions to offer a positive balance in the workplace.

And in a world of artificial intelligence, being in touch with our emotional responses is even more vital—it's our differentiator. So, let's all take a leaf out of Oprah's book and embrace our emotional, authentic self.

A WORD ABOUT ANXIETY

If you're in middle age, you may feel that anxiety is something of a modern disease. In my school years, I don't recall any instances at school where children were missing for a "mental health" day. But there are positive benefits in moving away from a "stiff upper lip" mentality and recognising anxiety for what it is.

Feeling anxious is a natural, built-in response to danger. A chemical reaction takes place in situations where we are fearful—often referred to as the fight, flight or freeze response. Today we find that running from that sabre-tooth tiger has been replaced by deadlines and unreasonable workloads.

Like any monster-under-the-bed syndrome, anxiety needs to be faced and acknowledged rather than suppressed. And we have modern techniques to deal with this modern danger—mindfulness, meditation apps, medicines (homeopathic or traditional)—and greater recognition for these requirements in the workplace.

Stress can be good for us. In her TED talk, Psychologist **Kelly McGonigal**[33] describes how it makes your heart pound, your breathing quicken and your forehead sweat. But while stress has been made into a public health enemy, new research suggests that stress may only be bad for you if you believe that to be the case.

McGonigal urges us to see stress as a positive and introduces us to an unsung mechanism for stress reduction: reaching out to others. So, try to put your arms around stress—and know when it's time to tell it to run off and play somewhere else.

A WORD ABOUT CONFIDENCE

Do you find confident people annoying? They can be, especially if it's about a topic that you know nothing about in front of people you'd like to impress. Of course, the truth is like many behaviours, confidence is a choice. We can all fool ourselves (and others) that we are confident if we set our minds to it (remember neuroplasticity!).

At work, gaining confidence relies on us feeling safe and secure and so much of that state of mind results from truly understanding ourselves and our "hot button" reactions.

The next time you feel a rising panic, ask yourself where that response comes from. Is it imposter syndrome? Or a childhood memory of being humiliated or under-prepared?

Discover the narrative behind those negative thoughts and recraft the story to acknowledge the new reality—you are experienced, you have a track record and you can be ready for anything.

CHAPTER 5

WHAT MIDLIFE EMPLOYEES SHOULD KNOW

Employed but unsettled—is this you?

Perhaps you've been in the same role for a while but just lost a promotion, gained a new boss you can't stand, or simply feel you've outgrown your current employer. Time to move on.

Let's take a deeper dive into the fundamentals for midlife employees to take a closer look at their career and hear how some people have changed their story and their work prospects.

QUICK FIX

- Few of us end up with the careers we started out with—and sometimes we stay too long in situations that are ill-suited to our personal values.

- It's good practice to question regularly what you want out of life and your work.

- Consider gaining a better understanding your own behaviours, prioritising communications and accepting that the only certainty is change.

- Switch up your thinking; techniques such as drama improvisation and NLP can help you embrace flexibility and respond better to challenging times.

- Read the stories of successful midlifers who changed course.

 to Who's been there?

Find out more

> "I'm getting too old for that," Hem said. "And I'm afraid I'm not interested in getting lost and making a fool of myself. Are you?"
>
> Source: Who Moved My Cheese? Dr Spencer Johnson

Connecting with resilience

While resilience might be the end game, it isn't a "one and done" pursuit. Let's say you've found your ideal role, but you're struggling under the constant burden of unrealistic deadlines, the unhelpful comments or attitude of a team member or boss or a sense of existential crisis that results in questioning your motivation and influencing a sense of unrest, even when you are at not at work.

As the earlier example of Vera Wang shows us, we may fall at the first hurdle in getting the right qualifications to become a solicitor or become hampered by a sports injury that blights our future career as an athlete.

For many, work "evolves" through trying different roles or getting a promotion that involves learning about a new industry or exploring a new geography. Often, people "follow the crowd" and are headhunted or recruited to reunite with former colleagues.

Sometimes, we just stay put because of personal circumstances, health matters, better-the-devil-you-know attitudes or simply because the job is a means to an end (where having money is more of a priority than personal fulfilment).

There is little doubt that the 2020 global pandemic upended all our working lives. From destroying livelihoods as person-to-person sales dried up or driving a permanent desire to lose the commute, COVID-19 opened the door to a new, unprecedented relationship with work and our working environment. Some people switched careers altogether; some became digital nomads; some questioned the quality of their lives and have yet to find the answers.

> **QUALIFICATIONS AND EXPERIENCE COUNT FOR NOTHING IF WE DON'T HAVE THE STAMINA TO FACE AND OVERCOME DIFFICULTIES OR CHANGE.**

In the last three decades, there have been many articles about burn-out as executives become immobilised by stress and overwhelmed by an inescapable sense of inadequacy or guilt. Trapped in psychological quicksand, extra working hours can lead to hospitalisation.[34] The strain of this weariness is nowhere more evidenced than in the NHS where post-pandemic staff said they were "exhausted from being exhausted" in a review of health and social care leadership.[35]

Women often carry the burden of childcare and caring for elderly relatives. Yet, unfortunately, too often, they overly compensate for male-driven environments and can become brittle and bullying. I will never forget the senior executive who insisted I work late into a Friday evening to finish a project, despite knowing that my mother was seriously ill (she died within a few months).

Or there was the time when a senior marketing director insisted I write three research reports from scratch in two weeks; to do a thorough job, the request was not reasonable, but the marketing director had a reputation for seeking out a scapegoat to hide her own planning and management failings and a certain amount of sadism in her dealings with junior staff. It is moments like these, where we may be under strain from a variety of factors, where resilience becomes a priority.

It is good practice to question regularly what you want out of life and your work. But we all know that decision making is best when it accommodates all the facts.

Resilience fundamentals

Here are some useful elements to consider as you wrestle with your career:

A need to understand your own behaviours: We've talked about the vital role of the brain and mindset in becoming resilient—gaining flexibility in your own thoughts (neuroplasticity) and the role of purpose (logotherapy).

But there are other in-built behaviours that can have a dramatic influence our thoughts and actions—not just affecting our resilience but our very survival. Today, this survival mechanism, characterised by fight, flight freeze or feign death responses, is tested less by the threat of being eaten by a wild animal and more by facing your boss in a difficult performance review, but the body's response can be just as dramatic.

One person who has studied stress responses in some detail is **Dr Stephen Porges**,[36] a distinguished American psychologist and neuroscientist. His research on the Polyvagal Theory[37] emphasises the role the autonomic nervous system plays—especially the vagus nerve, a superhighway that connects the heart, lungs, upper digestive tract, and other organs of the chest and abdomen—in regulating our health and behaviour.

He describes how safety, co-regulation, and connection are essential to a healthy human experience. For this reason, neuroscientist and coach Delphine Dépy Carron,[38] who co-runs the Institute of Neuroscience for the Transformation of Organisations (INTO),[39] focuses on informing workforces about the vagus nerve as she helps them to better harness their stress responses in periods of transformational change.

"Once people can better assess risk around how safe they feel at work, they can adapt and be more committed to their company's overall vision," Dépy Carron states. "In this way, organisations can help workers thrive in a more collective and connected way."

 to Find out more/Take charge of your well-being

Prioritising communications: It's interesting how often familiar phrases, as trite as they may seem, have a strong basis in fact. "A problem shared is a problem halved" or "two heads are better than one" may seem glib statements, but there is plenty of evidence to suggest that communicating with others is a spur for creativity, personal development and growth.

As a business writer for large corporates for many years, I have seen how the accent has long been on storytelling as an effective method for sharing marketing messages. Case studies are still considered to be more effective than sales brochures and the era of the influencer has highlighted how personal recommendation, even for someone unknown, can affect product sales dramatically.

Of course, the art of storytelling is an ancient one and can be applied even in the most difficult of circumstances, such as handling psychotherapy and the effects of trauma. What's important in any working situation is to keep those communication channels open—and clear.

Request to speak to your line manager. Involve the HR department where you can. Speak in confidence to other trusted colleagues. Share your concerns with appropriate third parties outside of employment.

Above all, make sure that you keep the communication channel open with yourself—be honest about how you are feeling. Consider documenting your thoughts on a regular basis (see the accompanying Workbook at www.nynclub.co.uk for useful exercises).

 WORKBOOK TIP: Exercise 3.2 Do your daily Wordres

Word games

There are plenty of examples where a lack of clarity in communications has led to a misunderstanding, sometimes with dramatic consequences. One of the most extreme examples of how poor phrasing can be open to interpretation is the report that led to the Bay of Pigs invasion.

If you're not familiar with this incident, it refers to Fidel Castro overthrowing the government in Cuba in the 1960s. Buoyed by his recent election win in the United States, President John F. Kennedy considered invading Cuba and overthrowing Castro—the prospect of communism and Soviet alliance so close to United States' shores was not an attractive one.

A report was crafted by the Joint Chiefs of Staff (JCS) who said such a plan had a "fair chance" of success. President Kennedy interpreted this statement as a "good chance" when in fact the JCS meant they thought it had a three times higher probability of failure than success.[40]

It begs the question: why didn't they explain their terminology? Why didn't President Kennedy or his staff check his interpretation? Above all, it reminds us once again that clarity in communications, especially those with such far-reaching consequences, is never a wasted effort.

The only certainty is change: When **Mahatma Ghandi** said: "Be the change you wish to see in the world" he could not have guessed it would be misappropriated by so many different professions and used to promote so many different causes. But the cornerstone of resilience is an adaptability to circumstances that means, to cite an oxymoron, change should be part of the status quo.

Today, there are so many tips and techniques and people's bookshelves, including my own, are groaning from self-help advice—from exploring happiness to asking who moved your cheese.

In a second jobseekers' course that is targeted more specifically toward students in education, 2B Ready uses improvisation comedy (commonly known as improv) to get students to think differently and break free of the confines of academic thinking. According to drama, improvisation and comedy coach **Alison Goldie**, improv is "the art of being completely OK with not knowing what you are doing".

Improv exercises are meant to be fun, but they also teach us about trust, the confidence to be yourself, and the power of saying "Yes" to opportunities. The human brain evolved around survival and reproduction. Yet, as we see in Maslow's hierarchy of needs, once basic needs are fulfilled we seek out more sophisticated outcomes.

In addition, the 2BR course employs short Neuro Linguistic Programming (NLP) exercises as brain training to handle future challenges. NLP is a study of how we do what we do; it teaches us that it's not what happens to you that makes a difference, but what you do with it. Neuro refers to the nervous system where our experience of the world enters using five senses: visual (seeing), auditory (hearing), kinaesthetic (touch), olfactory (smell) and gustatory (taste). Linguistic refers to the language used and programming refers to ways in which we consistently think or behave.

The two "fathers" of NLP are **John Grinder**, a professor of linguistics in California, and **Richard Bandler**, who had studied a range of subjects including Gestalt therapy (a form of psychotherapy focused on a person's present life and challenges rather than past experiences).

NLP is a philosophy and an attitude that is useful when your goal is excellence in whatever you do. According to the Association for NLP,[41] there are some presuppositions that form the foundation of NLP:

- **Have respect for the other person's model of the world.** We are all unique and experience the world in different ways. Everyone is an individual with their own special way of being.

- **The map is not the territory.** People respond to their "map" of reality, not to reality itself. How people make sense of the world around them is through the lens of their own personal experience; this means that an individual's perception of an event is different.

- **We have all the resources we need or we can create them.** These resources can be internal or external, which is a useful reminder; sometimes, believing this enables us to be better empowered in any situation.

- **Mind and body form a linked system.** Your mental attitude affects your body and your health and, in turn, how you behave.

- **If what you are doing isn't working, do something else.** Flexibility is the key to success.

- **Choice is better than no choice.** Having options can provide more opportunities for achieving results.

- **We are always communicating.** Even when we remain silent, we are communicating. Non-verbal communication can account for a large proportion of a message.

- **The meaning of your communication is the response you get.** While your intention may be clear to you, it is the other person's interpretation and response that reflects your effectiveness.

- **There is no failure, only feedback.** What seemed like failure can be thought of as success that just stopped too soon. With this understanding, we can stop blaming ourselves and others, find solutions and improve the quality of what we do.

- **Behind every behaviour there is a positive intention.** When we understand that other people have some positive intention in what they say and do (however annoying and negative it may seem to us), it can be easier to stop getting angry and start to move forward.

- **Anything can be accomplished if the task is broken down into small enough steps.** Achievement becomes easier if activities are manageable; NLP can help you learn how to analyse what needs to be done and find ways to be both efficient and effective.

Switching up your thinking using techniques such as improv and NLP can help to normalise change and introduce a flexible response to challenging times.

Who's been there?

Midlife is not only a time to reflect on your journey so far, but also a time to discover new horizons. Here are some examples of people who have decided to seize the day, either changing careers or taking charge of their career path.

Moving from the boardroom to the tasting room

Although born in the UK, **Sally Evans** has lived in France for half her life, working as a Global Marketing Director for a leading management consultancy firm. Despite a demanding role and raising two sons, approaching midlife Sally sought out a new challenge.

Without any prior knowledge of the wine industry, she bought a parcel of vines and some dilapidated buildings in the Fronsac region near Bordeaux and began renovating and creating a new wine chateau.

Now, her award-winning wine brand, Château George 7, appears in Michelin-starred restaurants and venues around the world. As a vintner and a mentor, she runs a successful wine and tourism business from the vineyard and has written a book "Make the Midlife Move"[42] that charts her journey.

"If ever there was a time to reveal your authentic self and realise your dream, it's in midlife, when the only thing stopping you is yourself," says Sally.

Slowing down to speed up change

For over a decade, **Gib Bulloch** led a team within one of the largest global consulting organisations—a corporate "guerilla movement" working deep within the system to try to change the system.

Against the odds, he created a not-for-profit inside one of the most profit-driven corporations in the world. Plaudits and promotions followed. But success came at a price: it ultimately cost him his job, his health and even his sanity as he found himself the unlikely resident of a psychiatric hospital.

After a period of deep reflection, in his mid-40s Gib changed course. He now runs the Craigberoch Business Decelerator, empowering purpose-driven intrapreneurs[43] to unlock organisational innovation and change. It's mission? To inspire and nurture an ecosystem of changemakers who will generate sustainable solutions to the world's greatest challenges.

"Our online and in-person events help people slow down, access their creativity and tap into their purpose so they can drive positive change in themselves, their organisations and local communities," says Gib.

CHAPTER 5

High-flyer recommends finding your tribe

Angela Fraser has a track record as a Bid Director, a complex and demanding role she's undertaken for a string of high-tech corporates. In her early 60s she took voluntary redundancy to plan her next opportunity, including launching her business Dragonfly Pursuit offering bidding services, primarily deal coaching.

Within a couple of years, her personal circumstances changed dramatically when her mother became ill, passing in 2023. Surfacing from grief and post-death practicalities and her own health scares, Angela realised she had "accidentally retired".

Undeterred and probing different avenues to "find her tribe", she's nearly completed a Philosophy and Psychology degree, volunteers as Marketing Director and coach for the Association of Proposal Management Professionals (APMP) and has even undertaken a thrilling wing walk in aid of charity.

"I know my skill set could benefit someone else and that's where I'm headed. I'm open and flexible to what's next and ready to take that step into the unknown—though it's unlikely to be onto another plane wing cruising at 700 feet!"

TRY NOW: Get to grips with the story you are telling yourself and understand if it serves any purpose. You know the old adage of facing down a monster that's chasing you in your nightmares? It's important to look your career history squarely in the eyes.

 WORKBOOK TIP:
Exercise 4.2 My career journey.

CHAPTER 6

THE ROLE OF THE NARRATIVE

We all have a story to tell—more than one—but rather than remembering the facts we may be hanging onto feelings that are unhelpful and skew the truth. Let's uncover the real you by getting down to the details of how narrative practice is applied in a therapeutic context and discovering how to get started to use it for work to reinvent your midlife career.

> **WORKBOOK TIP:** Take a look at Section 2 EMBRACING NARRATIVE PRACTICE for exercises that explore this topic further.

QUICK FIX

- Everyone has complexity in their lives. Narrative Practice helps us see the bigger picture, find hidden strengths, acknowledge achievements and better understand our experiences to positively influence our careers.

- Narrative Practice stems from the intellectual partnership and friendship of therapists **Michael White** and **David Epston**.

- Narrative Practice helps to organise the stories we tell ourselves through concepts that include externalising challenging situations, uncovering the narrative, contradiction and collaboration.

- This section explores Narrative Practice techniques, including the dot exercise, suitcase project, narrative maps, tree of life and outsider witness.

- Find out how to get started with Narrative Practice.

 to How to get started

Find out more

> "I write entirely to find out what I'm thinking, what I'm looking at, what I see and what it means."
>
> Joan Didion, The Year of Magical Thinking

As long as I can remember, words have mattered—from the succinct but sobering "satisfactory" on my school reports, to being told at 17 that I was pompous (courtesy of my French teacher in response to my poor translation efforts). But words can often develop into labels within a story we tell ourselves that becomes our defining path.

Storytelling has been essential to my day job. As a freelance business writer, I have been required to frame complex research content into a narrative that makes sense to executives in large corporations for nearly 30 years. But it wasn't until coming across the therapeutic application of Narrative Practice that I had given much thought to the influence of storytelling to bridge the gap between our personal lives and our approach to or at work—and the empowerment and improvement that could result from a better blend.

Described as a "passionate storyteller," you may be familiar with **Joseph Campbell**,[44] author of "The Hero's Journey" and credited as an inspiration for bringing mythology to a mass audience as well as influencing other writers and creatives such as John Steinbeck, Alan Watts and Film Director George Lucas. He's quoted for pithy statements such as "Follow your bliss" and "You are that mystery which you are seeking to know".

Campbell was also known to throw down the gauntlet at the end of his seminars asking questions such as: Are you going to go on the creative soul's quest or are you going to pursue the life that only gives you security? Are you going to follow the star of the zeal of your own enthusiasm? Are you going to live the myth or is the myth going to live you?

In later midlife, even as I type those questions, I am wishing he had asked me so much earlier in my career! Yet, Narrative Practice can show us that, whatever paths we take, there is a richness to our multi-storied lives.

Everyone has complexity in their lives and by acknowledging the different strands and how they knit together into an overall story, we can see the bigger picture, find hidden strengths, acknowledge achievements and better understand our experiences to positively influence our careers.

THERE IS RICHNESS TO OUR MULTI-STORIED LIVES.

As mentioned earlier, Narrative Practice stems from the intellectual partnership and friendship of family therapist Michael White and New Zealand therapist, David Epston.[45] Working together over many years, the two therapists invited people to express deep seated concerns or personal challenges. Using powerful storytelling techniques, they set about liberating those who feel stuck with thoughts or behaviours that are questionable, inaccurate or simply unhelpful along life's journey.

Narrative Practice concepts include:

1. Externalising challenging situations: White and Epston introduced the idea of externalising problems as early as the 1980s. When individuals view their problems as external influences rather than wrapped up with who they are, it's easier to address and manage their problems. In short, **"the person is not the problem. The problem is the problem."**

We've all had those moments where we describe our response to a situation in catastrophic terms—"I'm hopeless at X….", "I'll never be any good at Y…", "I've always been unlucky at work". Through a careful understanding of what's behind this language, Narrative Practice suggests it is possible to step back and separate from the problem and free yourself from judgment or blame.

For instance, with depression, gentle questioning can establish how long depression has been an influence in a person's life, when it started, why it started, what the real effects of the depression are (on the person, their relationships and others), and what helps to remedy the situation.

People often feel relieved by this deeper analysis because it helps them to disassociate from the labels they give themselves. So instead of saying "I am depressed" you may choose to say "I have depression"— it's a way of separating yourself from the condition and identifying depression as something you are experiencing, rather than something intrinsic to your nature.

In this way you can begin to imagine a life where depression reflects less who you are and is more a condition that is manageable—something you can overcome.

WE ARE ALL SHAPED BY OUR EXPERIENCES.

By separating our identities from problems which arise and viewing those problems more objectively, we can reclaim our narrative.

2. Uncovering the narrative: By examining and breaking down the key or recurring stories that tend to dominate our lives, we can uncover and deconstruct our assumptions and values that lie underneath.

In this way, we can see how certain beliefs are shaped by societal norms, cultural expectations, or personal history, and how these may limit our potential. Once you've deconstructed the story, a person is encouraged to "re-author" their narrative. This is not suggesting that you should fabricate your experiences or play "make believe" on a life you'd rather have had. But it is about viewing and articulating those challenging aspects of your life in a different light.

By creating new, more empowering stories that better align with what you value, what you hope to achieve and how you see yourself, you can gain a hopeful view of your life with rich possibilities that can help you move forward more positively.

As an aside, there's a great story that's surfaced in several places about a speaker who, about to launch into his presentation, reaches into his pocket and removes a 50-dollar bill from his wallet. He holds it up.

"By a show of hands," he says, "who would like this 50-dollar bill?" All hands shoot up.

"OK," he says, then crumples it up and asks "now, who would like it?"

Everyone signals they would gladly take the money. Then he drops the bill and steps on it, grinding it into the ground.

"Now, who would like it?" The note is filthy and barely recognisable but still all hands rise. The speaker smiles.

"You know what's just like this 50-dollar bill? Anyone?" No one answers.

Finally, the speaker gestures out to the crowd.

"You are. You see, no matter what I did to this bill you still saw the value in it. What happened to it didn't decrease its value; it's still worth US$50. The same is true of you, you will always have value".

We think struggle or hardship decreases our value—and sometimes we do feel diminished. But these are feelings, not facts. They don't have to define you. There's much we can gain from the challenges we face. Having weathered the storm, some part of you becomes stronger and more resilient.

3. Contradiction and collaboration: Countering a negative view of yourself means you can see yourself in a new, more positive way and that, in turn can lead to greater resilience and renewal. Collaboration lies at the heart of Narrative Practice—honed over many years of White and Epston sharing their ideas and experiences—and once the people they encountered believed they are the author of their own story, they were able to work with a therapist to reshape an existing narrative and co-create a new story.

Collaboration helps people to feel safe to expose their vulnerabilities and reassures them that they are not alone in finding answers to their distress. So far, Narrative Practice has been used in individual, couple or family therapy settings and the outcomes are widely documented by one of the key "homes" of Narrative Practice, The Dulwich Centre in Australia.[46] As well as offering courses on the topic, the centre has a range of resources[47] that explore the subject matter and its applications.

Narrative Practice has been equally applied in community settings, helping groups and communities to express the stories of the disadvantaged or where social justice is lacking. It is used by educators to support students on their learning journeys and organisations that are looking to define their culture or mission to a wide group of people.

Unlike traditional therapeutic relationships, the therapist is seen not so much a someone to interpret or solve the problem, but someone who works with the client to help them to gain control, building confidence and self-esteem along the way.

> BEING HEARD, SEEN AND UNDERSTOOD IS HIGHLY VALIDATING AND HONOURS YOUR LIVED EXPERIENCES.

Narrative Practice techniques

Let's take a closer look at some elements of Narrative Practice and how they might be applied in a work context:

Dot exercise: Established by **Jill Freedman** and **Gene Combs**, a dot exercise is being used to work with people to find new meaning in their lives, especially to improve their mental health. In a picture of a series of dots, a person is asked to imagine that each of the dots represents a life experience.

When they first start working with a therapist, people often have a single line that connects their life path so far; the therapist listens but can point out that this is one possible thread that connects these dots—there are other dots with multiple events outside of that story which are also representative.

By connecting those dots, possibly overlapping with the existing story but taking it in a different direction, people can find rich and complex meaning to their lives. The series of dots and connecting those dots differently speaks of multiple possibilities. Problematic stories can take on a whole new meaning when they are seen as just one strand of a multi-storied landscape. See the visual (Figure 3) of all the strands and how they represent the different stories that you tell yourself or others about yourself.

How to apply the dot exercise concept for work:

1. Look at the whole picture of your life's experiences and how events have influenced your career.
2. Consider that the strategy game you spent hours playing when you should have been doing household chores. It may be more relevant than you think—and could make all the difference to

your next job application where the company is looking for someone who can think and act strategically.

3. Don't box yourself in with one story about who you are. Some of the negative aspects of your story can also connect to positive outcomes and new directions.

4. Think about how to join and discover dots in your own life and the connections that you make between their performance and progress to help you in the future.

5. Map the dots to life and career defining events.

6. See how those events might overlap and how they might help to build out your work profile.

Figure 3. The dot exercise

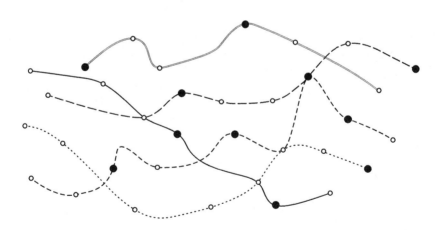

Each dot represents a milestone or important event. Our story links these events. But sometimes we connect only one combination of dots when other combinations are open to us.

 WORKBOOK TIP:
Exercise 2.1 Explore the dot exercise

Suitcase project: Ncazelo Ncube-Mlilo[48] is a Zimbabwean psychologist and narrative therapist living and working in South Africa. Inspired by the work of Glynis Clacherty and drawing on ideas from Sherri Osborn, she explains how a "Narratives in the suitcase"[49] project uses journey metaphors to assist child refugees as they migrate from rural areas to the city, seeking a better life.

These "children on the move" were often referred to in derogatory terms for having neglected their families and got into trouble, but the narratives in suitcase project helped to give these children richer descriptions of what they were pursuing—carrying suitcases not only implied the movement of the children, but also that they were carrying with them many valuable things.

Within the project, each child had an opportunity to make a suitcase using a cardboard box and was then encouraged to get creative by drawing or pasting pictures onto it, including a symbol of one thing they have had with them since embarking on their journey. The cases included reference to things that made them happy, favourite people or songs, artists and hobbies and what they are proud of.

Many children identified the hope for a better life, wanting to be better educated, seeking a bright future and wanting to help family members. The project offered an unprecedented opportunity to explore what mattered to them most and culminated in developing a banner identifying collective lessons learned along their journeys.

As one child said of the experience: "the suitcase is like my heart, and today I feel that I've been talking about the secret things that I have been thinking about, but I've never had a chance to talk about, because people could think I'm crazy".[50]

CHAPTER 6

How to apply the suitcase concept for work:

1. Identify what you already carry with going into a new work situation, including being honest about the "baggage" of workplace situations and scenarios that you may have failed to let go in the past.

2. Create stickers with descriptive words that can be placed onto your suitcase, whether they represent intended destinations or markers of what companies you've worked for in the past.

3. Understand what you carry around inside you that you can pack to be better prepared—there can be many valuable things and rich gifts, so make a list of all those things that travel with you into the workplace.

4. Develop your own "suitcase of capabilities" that represent where you are headed on your work journey. Resilience could be one key packable item!

WORKBOOK TIP:
Exercise 2.2 Explore the suitcase project

Narrative maps: A map of Narrative Practice is a structured guide that uses steps or questions to support a narrative conversation. These maps[51] are not rigid rules for practice, but using the maps can support practitioners in developing and deepening Narrative Practice skills.

Michael White, a major international figure in family therapy, had a lifelong fascination for maps that led him to look at them as a metaphor for his work with people who consulted him with a range of issues. White considered that geographical metaphors of land, topography and territories were a safe and reflective means to examine human processes—especially since they evoke the possibilities of travel in relation to steps taken and relational developments.

Most narrative maps have question areas and a recommended sequence for asking them—for instance, in trying to understand different aspects of identity, the conversation might progress from intentions and purposes (what you're aiming to do or achieve through a particular action) to values and beliefs (ways of acting or being that you feel are right at a particular time), then hopes and dreams (your ideas about how life or work could be), principles (a grander view of ways of acting and being that you believe we should all live by) and finally commitments, the principles that you stand for and that shape your actions.

> "We're the real countries. Not the boundaries drawn on maps with the names of powerful men."
>
> The English Patient, Michael Ondaatje

How to apply the narrative maps concept for work:

1. Identify what you are struggling with right now with respect to your work. If this problem were a person, what kind of person would they be? What would a drawing or painting of this problem look like?

2. Be clear on when the problem arose in your life and what areas of your working life is affects the most. How do you respond to this problem? What happens to your mood and relationships in the light of this problem? You can also consider whether it has affected how you see yourself as a person or how you see your future career mapping out.

3. Understand the impact on your values, whether they are compromised and think about how you can chart a different course and head into a different direction to resolve these challenges.

WORKBOOK TIP:
Exercise 2.3 Explore narrative maps

Tree of life: Another popular therapeutic tool in Narrative Practice toolkit is the Tree of Life.⁵² Created by Ncazelo Ncube-Mlilo (see the suitcase project mentioned earlier) and **David Denborough** it was intended to help individuals and communities to express their life stories and values in a way that fosters resilience, identity and empowerment.

Using the metaphor of a tree, people can represent different aspects of their lives and identity, giving them an opportunity to explore their past, present, and hopes for the future in a safe and structured way. It is often used with children, trauma survivors, and marginalised communities.

A tree, like a river, is one of the universal symbols of life and can help people dig deeper into their own lives through its associated properties: the roots, trunk, branches, leaves, fruits and buds. People are asked to draw their own tree to visualise and externalise their personal experiences.

Once drawn, they share their stories with others and discuss the meaning behind each part of their tree. Sometimes, individual trees are brought together to create a "forest" of trees, symbolizing the collective strength of the group or community.

How to apply the tree of life concept for work: This familiar metaphor offers a way to explore identity, relationships, and personal growth in a working context.

1. Draw a tree where the roots represent the strong influences shaping a career to date; the trunk represents skills and talents and how people have navigated their careers; the leaves signify the important relationships and influencers along the career journey; the fruits are personal achievements and the promotional help and the buds are hopes for the future.

2. By identifying how your career fits in the different areas of the tree, you can reframe your working life stories in ways that affirm your values and strengths, even when you are uncertain or unhappy about your prospects.

> **WORKBOOK TIP:**
> Exercise 2.4 Explore the tree of life

Outsider witness: an outsider witness is a third party who is an invited audience to a therapy conversation. This can help not only in linking third-party experiences to the conversation, but also often results in the emergence of new ideas and ways of tackling challenging situations or behaviours.

Outsider witnesses could be part of the person's existing community, such as family or friends, or they might be invited from outsider networks, like other professionals or people who have sought counselling consultations for similar difficulties.

The outsider witness can often have a unique view of the challenges faced by the patient which serve to give a new perspective. The process can often result into an easier transition for the patient to adopt new ways of approaching a problem in their daily lives.

In a sense, the reality of an outsider in the process helps to bridge the gap between the outsider world and the therapy room. Outsider witnesses are often affected by what they hear and, in turn, the person at the centre of the conversation can feel more seen and heard.

CHAPTER 6

How to apply the outsider witness concept for work: We all have different ways of living our lives, but this concept can be adopted in a working environment to benefit two perspectives—offering insights for the person who acts as an outsider witness as well as practical help the person experiencing challenges at work.

Outsider witness practices offer an opportunity to be creative in a safe space with people you trust.

WORKBOOK TIP:
Exercise 2.5 Explore outsider witness

CHAPTER 7

HOW TO GET STARTED

As we have seen, confidence and resilience are as much a part of job search as the practical capabilities, such as improving CVs and interview technique. Just as Narrative Practice brings hope and purpose in a therapeutic scenario, it can be applied to your everyday to ease your way out of challenging working situations.

 WORKBOOK TIP: Take a look at Section 3 CRAFTING YOUR STORY for exercises that explore this topic further.

TELL THE STORY

Many people tell me they find it difficult to write. But whether it's crafting an email on a complex topic or the introductory letters when seeking a job, we all have experience in translating inner thoughts into words.

The trick with Narrative Practice is making that part a muscle memory by making it a more regular activity. **Julia Cameron**, screenwriter and author of "The Artist's Way" suggests "morning pages"—writing three longhand pages first thing in the morning to brain dump swirling thoughts.

I confess I have never taken up the practice, but I have written a daily diary at night for the last 50 years, so I can confirm that habitual writing aids expressing your thoughts—and can be helpful when you want to verify certain events in your past later in life!

EVALUATE THE STORY

The older we get the easier it is to see the red threads, the connections and coincidences, that have taken our career or life in a certain direction. No experience is ever wasted, a fact that was perfectly illustrated by **Steve Jobs**' speech to Stanford University in 2005.

Jobs told graduating students how he dropped out of his studies at Reed college and ended up doing a calligraphy class on campus, learning "what makes great typography great". Little did he realise at the time that 10 years later, when designing his first computer, this calligraphic experience elements would influence the scale and variety of Apple's groundbreaking typography and fonts.

CHAPTER 7

REFRESH THE STORY

As we've seen, one of the key success factors in Narrative Practice is collaboration, so it's important to involve others to verify and refresh your story. Try sharing your work history and asking for input from those you trust and respect.

It could also be effective to talk to one person and have another as an outside witness, observing the conversation and adding suggestions that enable a different perspective. If the task seems too great, break it down to bite-sized chunks—consider honing on a particular job or a particular skill rather than trying to assess your whole career in one session.

To get started on your new narrative, you can take a moment to imagine what you feel success looks like if you disregard what other people think and don't think about the future. Imagine you are far more confident and certain of your success—would you act differently?

And if you had the freedom to choose what's next, what would that look like?

In terms of the commitment to the written word, the accompanying Nail Your Narrative Workbook suggests a daily word game to sharpen your messages. You may be familiar with the popular daily puzzle, Wordle. Its name was born out of the combination of Word and Puzzle. So, here's a derivation of that idea around nailing your narrative— Wordres is the art of telling your story in words to be more resilient.

It's a daily game where you think of a sentence in 12 words or less that describes how you are today. You write it down or record it (increasing the word count as you wish). Do this every day, without fail. If you are struggling to articulate what you feel, you could also play some words into ChatGPT and ask it to form a sentence for you (remind yourself about AI and its impact by returning to "The AI era forces us to be "more human" in the section "What midlife jobseekers should know".)

Through regular practice, Wordres can help you to explore your thoughts in the present moment and learn to articulate them in a succinct and meaningful way. It can also serve as positive reinforcement.

Finally, you can reauthor your life by running through statements that reflect the story you are telling yourself today, the people, places or experiences that influenced those statements, then reframing and reworking them, and reviewing the revised narrative as a daily habit. Take some time to see how your narrative has evolved after completing this exercise for 12 months.

TRY NOW: In an article in **Hello** magazine, January 2025, actor Ted Danson, reflecting on his long career, said: "Gravity will slow you down, but your expectations and desires and purposefulness and contribution to the world are still valid and as important. So don't isolate—keep going, no matter how difficult it may be. Keep going". Imagine yourself in your future role and be clear about what it looks like.

WORKBOOK TIP:
Exercise 4.7 My future's journey

CHAPTER 8

FUTURE-PROOF RESILIENCE

Job change is a holistic endeavour and affects far more than tidying up your CV. We're all work-in-progress, no matter what our age, but in midlife it can be harder to reset thoughts and attitudes to be in the right frame of mind for work. Think of resilience as a lifelong project. Read on for practical steps and fresh ideas for midlife reinvention.

 WORKBOOK TIP: Take a look at Section 4 STRUCTURING CHANGE for exercises that explore this topic further.

 **QUICK FIX**

- Self-doubt, fear and anxiety are all elements that creep in during periods of unemployment or being unhappy in your current role.

- Some practical steps that can help include recognising repeating patterns, calibrating your curiosity, taking charge of your well-being, seeking out structure, talking it out and keeping up.

- A quick LinkedIn Poll showed that ageism is alive and well.

- Is it time to consider new models for midlife working, such as silver internships? (Think: Robert de Niro in "The Intern".)[53]

Find out more

> "You only fail if you don't try. Doing new things requires a lot of strength, a lot of energy. It can be very tiring trying to make things happen, to push fears aside. It's much easier to go with the flow; that's what most people do. But it's not interesting".
>
> Iris Apfel, interior designer and global fashion icon

CHAPTER 8

If you've never come across **Iris Apfel**, I encourage you to look her up—she was many things and certainly interesting. Her fashion career began as an octogenarian and when she died at 102 in 2024, she was well-known for her colourful and highly accessorized style. Iris is a shining example of someone who followed her passion and ended up reflecting the zeitgeist.

But it's not always easy to hold onto your confidence if you're struggling to search for a job or deeply unhappy in one. Self-doubt is bound to creep in. Fear and anxiety that stem from constant rejection can colour your view of the world. Soaring rents and friends who want to eat out when your bank balance is far from healthy are other more practical causes of concern.

At times like this, it's important to be easy on yourself. It's not just a case of "keep calm and carry on"; try to keep heading in the right direction by actively considering the following:

RECOGNISE REPEATING PATTERNS.

CALIBRATE YOUR CURIOSITY.

TAKE CHARGE OF YOUR WELL-BEING.

SEEK OUT STRUCTURE.

TALK IT OUT.

KEEP UP.

Recognise repeating patterns: Tasks that are both laborious and futile are often described as Sisyphean, referencing Greek mythology where Sisyphus was punished by the gods to roll an immense boulder up a hill—only for it to roll back down every time it neared the top—and forced to repeat this action for eternity.

Although the whole process of job applications can sometimes seem Sisyphean, it only takes one next stage interview to convert that effort into a positive result. Similarly, within an organisation a change of leadership or circumstances can reveal opportunities that may have seemed impossible beforehand.

Sometimes you need to change up existing habits to play your part in prompting these shifts. Prepare yourself for where you want to be not necessarily where you are. The important thing is to be ready and resilient enough to stay the course so you can seize that day when it arrives.

Calibrate your curiosity: It's important to find a balance between following every social media post and being up-to-date and interested in what's happening with others. Maintain an active interest in the stories of people you admire or wish to emulate while being kind to your own efforts.

Enjoy those moments where you feel uplifted by a positive response to an application or you a receive a rejection that also lists the positive impact your interview made on the company or feedback at work that recognises your contribution.

Listen to your heart and not only enjoy a healthy approach to introspection but also be aware of the essential nature of outrospection. As **Roman Krznaric** says on his book about empathy: "We should create a new Age of Outrospection where we find a better balance between looking inwards and looking outwards…I mean the idea of discovering who you are and how to live by stepping outside yourself and exploring the lives and perspectives of other people".[54]

Joining a professional network such as LinkedIn is one way of maintaining an active interest in the choices and journeys of others.

Get real, people

Be aware that in any research of social platforms you will need to get past a fair amount of sycophancy and showboating. I recommend you avoid reading any posts that start with "I don't usually write this kind of post, but…" cue an over-indulgent boast of a recent act of philanthropy or generosity.

You may also have to temper your incredulity at the behaviours of former employers who suddenly receive gushing reviews from their colleagues now they've moved on to another company that could be a good stepping stone for their own careers.

While it may appear many people are having a road to Damascus moment about life, the Universe and everything, the truth is more likely to be what it is for the rest of us—they're just doing the best they can day-to-day.

There is much virtue in getting the job done without trying to impress the rest of the world; constantly seeking validation from people who are unlikely to ever know you up close and personal is a fast-track to dissatisfaction and unease.

At the end of the day, there is no greater service we can give people than being our authentic selves—and sometimes that means keeping things to ourselves.

> "The elevator to success is out of order. You'll have to use the stairs… one step at a time".
>
> **Joe Girard**, American salesman, motivational speaker, and author

Take charge of your well-being: There are too many avenues that explore well-being, mental and physical, to mention here, but it's good to know that these topics are far more out in the open and up for discussion. According to nutritionist and author of "DO Nutrition" **Sarah Bayliss**[55] there are five pillars to a healthy life: Nutrition, Sleep, Movement, Relationships, Stress Management. Simple? It's challenging to get all five right.

Much has been said about the importance of sleep and the benefits of meditation. Sleep is one of the areas of your life that you can control, so experiment to find out what is right for you. Advice varies, but adults between the ages of 26 and 64 are expected to get between seven and nine hours of uninterrupted sleep each night according to the National Institute on Aging. Doctors recommend avoiding screen time up to an hour before you go to bed, but it is helpful to play meditative apps, such as Calm, to wind down your working day.

Daily podcasts from Calm with presenters such as **Jay Shetty** and **Tamara Levitt** can breed a soothing familiarity that can be highly effective. Also, try mixing things up. Work or work search can seem like a hamster wheel so breaking with your traditional patterns to do something different can give you the creative boost you need. It doesn't have to mean a full-blown two-week holiday to Ibiza. Taking a step back with a morning or day of non-routine activities—taking a walk or listening to music—can do wonders for your mindset.

In an era of personalised healthcare, where drugs are being designed to map to an individual's DNA, it's important to recognise your own responses, triggers, and working wellness. And when you have that balance right and find the right opportunity, don't allow imposter syndrome to take hold. Your career is in your hands.

Seek out structure: It can be a shock to be unemployed after years of money flowing in and out in harmony (or at least, in a manageable way). Full-time work can be all-consuming, but it drives an element of routine that can leave you feeling rudderless once it has gone; it's easy to drift.

If you like scheduling and order, then tick box lists could be the answer for you. Keep to a schedule of some kind or another by documenting your tasks. Identify what you need to do along with things you may want to do but don't seem to find the time to complete. Set yourself some targets and even deadlines and feel satisfied by meeting them.

You could also develop a new accountability with a friend or partner, arranging to meet or speak regularly to discuss those "to do's." Set your alarm daily and make ready as if you're going to work to avoid the "midday pyjama syndrome" to retain some sense of working normality.

Talk it out: Oscar Wilde, known for his pithy wit, said "I often have long conversations all by myself and I am so clever that sometimes I don't understand a single word of what I am saying."

Talking to yourself may be one way to keep the art of conversation alive, but there are many indications that upcoming generations are more comfortable with digital methods of communication than they are face-to-face.

Indeed, efforts to get pupils talking to each other at schools has resulted banning mobile phones during the school day. For one school in Plymouth, UK, the justification was that 88% of local employers said communication was the most important skills, but with many breaks being used to scroll or surf, pupils were losing the art of conversation.

Talking can also be a path to resiliency; learning how to avoid conflict or remain calm or indifferent are worthwhile qualities in companies where you are bound to come across people who have a different set of values.

Years ago, there was a phrase thrown around in the school playground (which sounds very old fashioned now) when someone was being mean that said: "Sticks and stones may break my bones. But words shall never hurt me". But in many ways, this is far from true.

Words can be very hurtful and, thanks to the internet, highly public, and we should all be considerate about how we handle difficult conversations. Open communication channels is a good start.

Keep up: It seems obvious to say, but it is especially important in midlife to keep up with the technologies, attitudes and conversations that are happening in the world. It's all too easy to become "stuck in our ways" and want to repeat patterns of behaviour that have worked for us in the past. This is not about having a midlife crisis, or the old tropes of buying a sports car and dressing like a teenager. Instead, it is a question of paying attention to what is going on around us and **embracing technological and societal shifts**.

As mentioned in "The AI era forces us to be "more human" in the section "What midlife jobseekers should know", AI is just one of many technological advances that are reshaping our human experiences, inside the workplace and outside of it. In 2025, we have yet to see the full scope and scale of its impact (despite my own personal reminder last year with the loss of a 30-year career to AI software).

Keep up by **educating yourself about new technologies** through different channels, such as the library, magazines like *The New Scientist* or educational channels online. There is so much available free of charge if you plug some words into a search engine (although bear in mind opinion bias and unsubstantiated claims).

Of course, books are a great source of insight, too. New content is being published all the time reflecting the latest trends and research studies. But taking a pulse of what's happening in the world doesn't have to be restricted to academic discourse or a reliance on news programmes. While I wouldn't suggest entering the confusing maelstrom of ideas (and occasional ugliness) that makes up social media, populist programmes from **television or streaming services reflect the zeitgeist**. Many of my friends are horrified that I am an avid watcher of "Love Island", for instance, the franchise reality show where single people stay in a villa abroad and couple up to avoid elimination. Despite being carefully curated and some coaching clearly taking place, it offers unique insight into the motivations of a group of 20- to 25-year-olds (and is worth watching for Iain Stirling's witty narration alone).

While this is not a recommendation in itself, keeping up with today's youth, perhaps **volunteering for a youth group** or helping out at a local school, can be hugely beneficial to boost your own credibility and instincts in a crowded marketplace—there's much to be said for learning from the curiosity, naivety or fearlessness of the young.

Another important way to stay relevant and resilient is to **seek out coaching or mentoring** help. Such services have been proven to open the door to the kind of resilience that has influenced careers—*Forbes* reported a study that found that 75% of executives say mentoring has been critical to their career development.[56] Whether you want to address your confidence, focus on the future or simply discuss your motivations with a third party, mentoring and coaching can revitalise your thinking.

As mentor **Andy Lopata** comments.

> "Whatever we try to achieve, it becomes easier with the help and support of other people. Having a mentor, or a team of mentors, whose judgment and experience you trust, gives you the benefit of people who will have your back and help you reach your full potential. Good mentors will challenge and hold you accountable, help you see possibilities and opportunities you might not otherwise have considered, help you fight off imposter syndrome, lift you when you're down, navigate challenging hurdles and guide you on your journey.
>
> Andy Lopata, co-author of *The Financial Times Guide to Mentoring* and host of *The Connected Leadership Podcast*.

Silver interns for hire

Many of the people who attend the 2B Ready post-education jobseeker courses are midlifers; typically, these candidates have a wealth of experience but for various reasons, such as redundancy or burnout, they are looking for a fresh start.

Research from the hotel and resort chain Hilton[57] found that 73% of over 50s are considering changing their working patterns to allow them to fulfil their dreams to travel, while more than a quarter of those who have children are looking to increase their working hours or change career paths now that their kids have left home. There are benefits for the whole company in having a diverse workforce.

The research found that 60% of over 50s said they can learn from working with those younger than themselves and more than three quarters (77%) of Gen Z respondents said they can learn from older colleagues, with leadership (44%) and problem solving (40%), communication (39%) and organisational skills (39%) being areas most cited where over 50s excel.

It's just one study but serves as a reminder that an older candidate can bring rich rewards to a company and its workforce. As a result, 2B Ready is proposing to our local community that we draw together a group of midlife candidates who are available for "silver internships", temporary periods of employment for three-, six- or 12-months, to bring much-needed skills and experience for short periods at a suitable cost.

Silver interns could undertake a one-off project or serve a broad number of departments in a range of tasks. In this way, companies can benefit from experienced hires and midlifers can make an effective contribution without being subjected to unacknowledged age bias.

In three quick polls I sent out via LinkedIn, targeted to midlifers, I wanted to discover how they were feeling about their job search journeys and what impact they thought their age may be having on the process. Perhaps unsurprisingly, when asked "What phrase best sums up your job search journey so far?" 46% said "hard work; so far unrewarding" and a further 31% said "the worst my career has seen".

Also, 71% agreed that age was likely to have a negative effect in securing their next job. Ways to improve their job search were fairly evenly split between "hearing from likeminded others" (30%), better recruitment feedback (30%) and "anything, I'm open to it all (41%), indicating most people searching for a job are prepared to face the future, welcoming a little help along the way.

An article in *The Telegraph* explores these issues. Examples of people in their late 50s and 60s painted a bleak picture of bias, made worse by automated application tracking systems and algorithms. Candidates that attempted to be flexible, applying for junior roles on less money, still experienced a closed door and found that the constant rejection was impacting their self-esteem.

As one candidate summed up: "After six months of tumbleweed, it got to the point that I had to stop job-hunting for the sake of my mental health. I felt completely invisible".[58]

TRY NOW: Be honest with yourself; change is hard and sometimes what we believe to be true fights back. Break routine habits and thinking with unplanned activities, like a spontaneous fishing trip, dancing to your favourite Spotify playlist in the kitchen or phoning a friend you've been meaning to speak to in a while. Remind yourself of those past hobbies or activities that bring you joy.

 WORKBOOK TIP:
Exercise 4.3 Chart your emotional journey.

CHAPTER 9

FIVE STEPS TO NAIL YOUR NARRATIVE

So, you have read about the techniques and how to apply them—but can you find a way to make your new reframed you less of a "to do" and more integral to your daily life? Let me guide you through five practical steps that can encourage the use of storytelling as a positive technique in your midlife career transformation.

QUICK FIX

- Narrative Practice can reinforce our strengths, increase our self-awareness and encourage flexibility and inclusivity.

- Five ways to grow Narrative Practice in your life include:

  - Be open to possibilities: Take a step forward, even if it isn't obviously the intended direction.

  - Make progress with purpose: Learn how to be useful—embrace experiences that connect to what matters.

  - Pay it forward: Be generous in sharing your skills and talents for the good of others.

  - Create a new normal: Find the magic in your day by mixing up standard practices.

  - Be the story: Regularly reset and reinvent to welcome your changing narrative.

- Download the Nail Your Narrative Workbook for more.

 WORKBOOK TIP: Take a look at Section 4 STRUCTURING CHANGE for exercises that explore this topic further.

CHAPTER 9

Find out more

We all have a story. But as **Ngozi Adichie Chimamanda** said in her TED talk[59] some 15 years ago, there's danger in adopting or assuming a single story. Born in Nigeria, Ngozi found people's assumptions about her life, capabilities and craft were often distorted and negative. She recognised that this was often a result of baked in assumptions about Nigeria and its people. She commented: "show a people as one thing, as only one thing, over and over again and that is what they become".

Now an author and an authentic voice for her homeland, Ngozi says the single story creates stereotypes—and the problem with stereotypes is not that they are untrue, but that they are incomplete. She sums up: "When we reject the single story, when we realise that there is never a single story about any place, we regain a kind of paradise".

Wouldn't we all like to be working in paradise? I believe it starts by acknowledging what we offer to the world and that process begins with better understanding and articulating who we are. We may well need to assume a new kind of confidence, even if that's a "fake it 'til you make it" kind.

We need to know our value and be clear on the values of others. Above all, telling our story to chart our work journey demands resilience. Introducing storytelling and refreshing the narrative that is told can **reinforce our strengths** and prompt alternative stories to build on that resilience and empower us to take control of our lives.

Narrative Practice can also **increase our self-awareness**. By exploring and deconstructing our narrative we can better understand the influences that are shaping who we are. Narrative Practice can **encourage flexibility and inclusivity** as we embrace different cultures and social behaviours to get the best that true diversity has to offer.

Here are some final takeaways for jobseekers and workforces alike that can influence nailing your narrative:

	1.	Be open to possibilities	Take a step forward, even if it isn't obviously the intended direction.
	2.	Make progress with purpose	Learn how to be useful—embrace experiences that connect to what matters.
	3.	Pay it forward	Be generous in sharing your skills and talents for the good of others.
	4.	Create a new normal	Find the magic in your day by mixing up standard practices.
	5.	Be the story	Regularly reset and reinvent to welcome your changing narrative.

1. **Be open to possibilities: Take a step forward, even if it isn't obviously the intended direction.** Let me remind you of the popularised song from the musical Annie where her brimming positivity promises "the sun will come out tomorrow". Are you feeling instantly annoyed or hopeful at the prospect?

Procrastination is popular but it is important to persevere and expect better outcomes. Whether we're in a job or looking for one, we may hold out for the "best" job or the "right" job—but all experience is good experience and sometimes a role that isn't obviously what we were aiming for takes us down an unexpected path with rich benefits. The story we tell ourselves is a significant influencer here.

As the Narrative Practice approach suggests, we should stop measuring our lives according to what certain social norms say life *should* be about. Our identities are made up, and continually being made up, of many (sometimes contradictory) stories⁶⁰ and there is no "right" path, just the one we choose to take. Remember the wise words of 12th century Sufi and Persian Poet, Rumi: "As you start to walk on the way, the way appears".

2. **Make progress with purpose: Learn how to be useful —embrace experiences that connect to what matters.** Often the purpose behind finding work is obvious— the necessary income to live comfortably. But that work will be far more fulfilling if we look for the meaning behind what we are doing.

According to the psychiatrist **Carl Jung**: "Meaning makes a great many things endurable, perhaps everything." We can find meaning even in jobs that we don't enjoy doing, but we should seek out experiences that connect us to the things that matter. Step back and consider your whole self and what qualities you bring to bear.

> 💡 **WORKBOOK TIP:** Checklists for change exercises 4.2 to 4.7

Think about the Narrative Practice suitcase exercise and chart your own journey by detailing all the people who have influenced your career to date, the things that interest you and what passions drive you forward. Ask yourself what you want to carry with you as you progress. Discard anything you may have been lugging around in the past which is no longer useful and save some room to carry the new and improved experiences going forward.

3. **Pay it forward: Be generous in sharing your skills and talents for the good of others.** We're all familiar with an airline's flight training request to "put your oxygen mask on first" if you need air during a crisis. The idea is

that, even with small children, if you run out of oxygen you cannot help anyone else until you help yourself.

In the study referenced earlier by Stanford University's **Kelly McGonigal**[61] about 1,000 adults in the United States were asked how much stress they had experienced in the last year and how much time they had spent helping out friends, neighbours or people in their community. The study found that every major stressful life experience, like financial difficulties or family crisis, increased the risk of dying by 30%—except for people who spent time caring for others, who showed zero increase. She concluded: "When you choose to view your stress response as helpful, you create the biology of courage, and when you choose to connect with others under stress, you can create resilience".

Train your brain toward positivity and purpose so you have "excess stamina" to advise others. Be aware of your own mental health and wellbeing so that you can be empathetic toward those who are struggling. Whatever your career trajectory, plan on the satisfaction of giving back, whether as a cheerleader to a friend in distress, a mentor to someone at work or as a willing pair of hands volunteering for a local charity.

In a quote attributed to the UK's illustrious Prime Minister, **Winston Churchill**: **"We make a living by what we get, we make a life by what we give"**. As a storytelling exercise, write down some of the ways you've helped others in the past or ways that you could help in the future. Consider how you could use channels, such as social media, to encourage and inspire, rather than using them purely as a vehicle to self-promote or critique others.

4. **Create a new normal: Find the magic in your day by mixing up standard practices.** Routine can be a necessary evil, especially when you are trying to keep many balls in the air at once. Actively make an effort to avoid

static or repetitive practices by introducing new experiences or changing the order of how you do things.

It's so easy to push on with projects even when your brain and body are telling you otherwise. I cannot tell you how many times in my writing career I may have been wrestling with a topic or paragraph and finally decided to get away from the desk to make a cup of tea—only to have a eureka moment that solves the challenging text.

Sometimes that break in sedentary posture can be enough. At other times, you may need to put some distance between you and the task beyond the metaphorical. Doing things differently can inspire different ideas. Our brain is always seeking out patterns and delights in well-worn behaviours. Try to wrong foot the brain and set a different intent. Instead of taking your normal journey to work, take a mode of transport or recalculate the route.

If you are seeking work, consider an exercise recommended by **Martha Beck** in her book "Find Your North Star"; visit your local library and wander through the shelves without any specific intention. See whether some sections or books draw your attention; it's the same kind of curiosity you used to feel when you were a child whenever something interesting passed your way. It can be subtle and easily ignored. Don't ignore it! Pick five books that give you the strongest tug and take a deeper look through them, noticing what you find interesting. Looking at topics in this way can often be a seed to something much more interesting.[62]

5. **Be the story: Regularly reset and reinvent your narrative to better manage change.** Let me stress again, Narrative Practice is not recommending that you live a fake life or fail to face challenging situations by pretending they didn't happen. It is about changing your relationship with your past to influence your future.

Accept your life with all its ups and downs and channel the good stuff that can help you meet your personal and professional goals. Consider yourself as your life's work. Long-term partnerships often suffer from one person changing and evolving and the other remaining "set in their ways". But we can also suffer from having a static image of ourselves.

Sometimes, events can trigger a response that takes you right back to the primary school playground (and indeed, sometimes working a corporate environment can seem like a primary school playground!) In the same vein as understanding that we can often only change ourselves, not the situation, we should aim to be the miracle in our own lives.

Take time to regularly reset and reinvent your approach to reflect changing times and desires. Consider starting the day with a mantra to set your intentions. Say this preferably out loud as soon as you wake (yes, even before you have reached for your phone) and say it as if you mean it. Here is a sample of a mantra; you can amend to suit your personal circumstances, intentions and preferences:

IN THE MORNING

I welcome the day.

I embrace energy and enthusiasm.

I open my heart to happiness.

I seek out success

I am ready and resilient

Then at the close of the day, consider how you can recognise your desires for tomorrow. There are many variations on the Buddhist Metta prayer (loving kindness meditation) but try this version in its simplest form.

The recommendation is that you first ask for these things for yourself, then you focus on someone you love ("may my son be safe" etc), then you imagine you are saying it to the whole world ("may everyone be safe").

IN THE EVENING

May I be safe.

May I be happy.

May I be healthy.

May I be at peace.

TRY NOW: Avoid overwhelm by chunking challenges and prioritising actions. As a former wise boss of mine used to say: "Rome wasn't built in a day"; don't beat yourself up every time you miss a deadline or are rejected from what seemed to be a shoo-in role. Taking just one of the five steps noted above is a worthwhile start and can help to progress reshaping your story.

WORKBOOK TIP:
Exercise 1.5 Be Yourself.

CHAPTER 10

SUCCESSFUL STORIES

Finally, some closing thoughts on making your own storytelling practices a success and a movie ending to make you smile.

We've all heard stories of friends or friends of friends who managed to slip into their career destiny from an early age. I have a friend whose son declared at three years old he would be a pilot and, indeed he is an excellent one (with the recording of his real-life engine failure incident being used to train many other pilots, too). But there are many other people, and I include myself, who have drifted into a profession and simply made the best of it.

In midlife hindsight, many of the choices we make are based on pure practicality—wanting your work to be flexible enough to be there for your family or a desire to live in a certain part of the country.

But we should also recognise that as the author of our own stories, we can get in our own way. We do this through procrastination or analysis paralysis (I am a living example of both) and, sometimes, through internalising (that inner dialogue), when the answers lie in release and expression, to ourselves and others.

What if we could adjust our storytelling more regularly to adapt our working conversations? What if we could review and reassess that changing story to get closer to a fulfilling working environment, first time, every time?

ISN'T IT TIME TO RECOGNISE AND ACCEPT THAT WE ARE MANY THINGS, NOT ONE THING— AND THAT IS A POSITIVE BENEFIT IN THE WORKPLACE?

The impact of Narrative Practice on individuals and communities, has proven to be profound. So, isn't it time to shake off the invisible cloak of midlife with authentic storytelling? As we've seen, neural pathways can be reimagined.

According to cognitive scientist **Lera Boroditsky**,[63] our language shapes the way we think, so if those thoughts are negative, it's worth considering how we can reimagine our narrative to heal, grow and respond to changes in our working lives—and continue to make our mark in the world.

I started this book sharing my secret passion for predictably happy films. Aside from the formulaic Christmas versions I mentioned, there is also a catalogue of (often) black and white films from the 1930s and 1940s that fall into a similar category of refreshingly straightforward light entertainment. I'm talking about the dance and musical era, such as movies from the legendary Busby Berkeley, Irving Berlin or Rodgers and Hart (or Hammerstein) featuring household names like Judy Garland, Frank Sinatra, Gene Kelly or the twinkle-toed Fred Astaire and Ginger Rogers.

Many of the songs in these musicals had achingly simplistic lyrics but, coupled with the storyline and dancing skills, can still be relevant today. So, I will leave you with a few lines from an enduring tune by songwriters **Jerome Kern** and **Dorothy Fields**[64] and, if you know it, I encourage you to sing along—and take heart from the sentiment:

Nothing's impossible, I have found
For when my chin is on the ground,
I pick myself up, dust myself off,
Start all over again.

Don't lose your confidence if you slip.
Be grateful for a pleasant trip,
And pick yourself up; dust yourself off;
Start all over again.

TRY NOW: In her TED Women talk, the actress **Jane Fonda** compared the process of reframing your thinking to resetting a thermostat, saying: "it's not having experiences that make us wise. It's reflecting on the experiences that we've had".[65] It may seem onerous but take the time to reflect and refine your story. Schedule it. Book a meeting with yourself, today. You could be amazed at the stories you discover.

Acknowledgements

Heartfelt appreciation to my son, Alex, for his encouragement in producing this book. In addition, my grateful thanks go to:

- Angela Fraser who pored over the manuscript and provided insightful and detailed comments to enhance your reading experience.

- Sally Evans, a role model for resilience and success.

- Kinga Stabryla for her patience and valuable advice around book publishing.

- Isobel Cogley, Julia Dunne, Jean Scoot; thanks for always listening.

- Dr Delphine Dépy Carron for introducing me to narrative practice and offering her valued advice.

- Upton Vale Baptist Church and Tony Hynes for supporting 2B Ready and Suzanne Wesley for being the best Programme Lead anyone could wish for.

I would also like to thank you, dear reader, for sparing some of your precious time and energy to read (or JUMP) through this book. It's easy to become sceptical in midlife and, since we all have different experiences and see the world through an individual lens, there are likely to be some passages you've read where you've snorted in derision, baulked at the idea or simply spluttered: "I don't agree. What is this woman talking about?" I want to assure you that my inner critic is alive and well and barely contained, so I hear you. Know that the sincere intentions behind "Nail Your Narrative" are to be humble, helpful and hopeful for the human spirit. Let's start there.

Further reading

- To learn more about Narrative Practice, see the Dulwich Centre: A gateway to narrative therapy and community work https://dulwichcentre.com.au/

- For information on 2B Ready courses visit https://www.2bready.co.uk

- For more on Upton Vale Baptist Church visit https://www.uptonvale.org.uk/

- For more on Viktor Frankl's Logotherapy visit https://viktorfranklamerica.com/

To access the "Nail Your Narrative Workbook" and keep in touch visit www.nynclub.co.uk

Endnotes

1 https://www.gettysburg.edu/news/stories?id=79db7b34-630c-4f49-ad32-4ab9ea48e72b

2 WHO, March 2021. https://www.who.int/news/item/18-03-2021-ageism-is-a-global-challenge-un

3 Neuro refers to the neurons and neural networks in our brain that process our thoughts and behaviours and plasticity is the ability to change and adapt and reorganise those thoughts and behaviours, rewiring our brains to think differently or tackle tasks differently.

4 "Degrading: we've got good degrees but we can't find good jobs," September 8, 2024, *The Sunday Times*

5 https://www.mooc.org/

6 https://www.skillsforcareers.education.gov.uk/

7 Emotional intelligence: the essential skillset for the age of AI, CapGemini, 2019.

8 Int J Aging Hum Dev. Author manuscript; available in PMC: 2017 May 24.

9 Capgemini Research Institute, Emotional Intelligence Research, Executive Survey, August–September 2019, N=750 executives; Employee Survey, August–September 2019, N=1,500 employees. Executives: refers to senior management, mid management and HR, Employees: refers to employees in non-supervisory roles.

10 https://thehomeofficelife.com/blog/work-from-home-statistics

11 *HR News*. September 9, 2021. https://hrnews.co.uk/survey-reveals-81-of-younger-workers-fear-loneliness-from-long-term-home-working/

12 https://www.dailymail.co.uk/news/article-12698491/Red-Arrows-pilots-women-property-predatory-behaviour-widespread-normalised-probe.html

13 https://www.bbc.co.uk/news/uk-england-york-north-yorkshire-61512811

14 Why curiosity may kill the cat but can save your brain and your future. https://en.delphinedepycarron.com/article-serious-game

15 https://www.ons.gov.uk/employmentandlabourmarket/peopleinwork/earningsandworkinghours/bulletins/genderpaygapintheuk/2023

16   https://www.mckinsey.com/featured-insights/diversity-and-inclusion/women-in-the-workplace

17   Women and the UK economy, March 2024. https://commonslibrary.parliament.uk/research-briefings/sn06838/#:~:text=In%20the%20UK%2C%2016.06%20million%20women%20aged%2016,women%20were%20employed%20than%20in%20the%20year%20before.

18   https://www.youtube.com/watch?v=Ij07Hk00Xsc

19   People are worried that AI will take everyone's jobs. We've been here before, *MIT Technology Review*, January 27, 2024. https://www.technologyreview.com/2024/01/27/1087041/technological-unemployment-elon-musk-jobs-ai/

20   The Future of Jobs report 2023. https://www.weforum.org/publications/the-future-of-jobs-report-2023/digest/

21   Focusing, How to gain direct access to your body's language, Eugene T. Gendlin

22   https://www.scientificamerican.com/article/the-adult-brain-does-grow-new-neurons-after-all-study-says/

23   https://www.simplypsychology.org/brain-plasticity.html#:~:text=Learning%20and%20new%20experiences%20cause%20new%20neural%20pathways,brains%20continue%20to%20show%20plasticity%20due%20to%20learning.

24   https://www.amazon.co.uk/gp/video/detail/B097NQ4SRY/ref=atv_hm_hom_c_Wxw9N3_5_1

25   Goleman, Daniel (1996), Emotional Intelligence, London, Bloomsbury Publishing plc

26   https://awaken.com/2024/02/debunking-the-myth-of-the-10000-hours-rule-what-it-actually-takes-to-reach-genius-level-excellence/

27   Grant, Adam (2023) Hidden potential, London, WH Allen

28   Adam Grant on How to Reach New Heights, *The Wharton Magazine,* Fall/Winter 2023. https://magazine.wharton.upenn.edu/issues/fall-winter-2023/adam-grant-on-how-to-reach-new-heights/

29   https://brenebrown.com/about/

30   https://www.businessballs.com/communication-skills/mehrabians-communication-theory-verbal-non-verbal-body-language/

31   Names have been changed to protect the individuals

32   Oprah Winfrey This is the moment my job ended and my calling began, April 1, 2019, CNBC https://www.cnbc.com/2019/04/01/how-oprah-winfrey-found-her-calling.html?msockid=22b46f01c9cb66f42cdc7cd4c85c67df

ENDNOTES

33   McGonigal, Kelly (2015, May) How to make stress your friend [Video]. TED Conferences

34   "When Executives Burn Out," July-August 1996, *Harvard Business Review*, https://hbr.org/1996/07/when-executives-burn-out

35   "Tired of being exhausted: seven key actions for leaders in the NHS workforce crisis," February 2022, https://www.kingsfund.org.uk/insight-and-analysis/blogs/tired-of-being-exhausted-seven-key-actions-leaders-nhs-workforce-crisis

36   https://www.linkedin.com/in/stephen-porges-6514877b/

37   https://www.polyvagalinstitute.org/whatispolyvagaltheory

38   https://en.delphinedepycarron.com/

39   www.institut-into.com.

40   What were you thinking? Biases and Rational Decision making, Thomas, Ted and Rielly, Robert J. https://thesimonscenter.org/wp-content/uploads/2017/08/IAJ-8-3-2017-pg98-105.pdf

41   https://anlp.org/knowledge-base/presuppositions-of-nlp

42   https://www.sallyevans.co.uk/makethemidlifemove

43   Intrapreneurs are those who apply entrepreneurial principles to develop innovations or ideas that create change within their corporate organisations.

44   Joseph Campbell, The Hero's Journey

45   The Dulwich Centre, Australia. https://dulwichcentre.com.au/

46   https://dulwichcentre.com.au/about-dulwich-centre/

47   https://dulwichcentre.com.au/resources/

48   Presentation at the International Narrative Therapy and Community Work Conference in March 2013

49   https://storynet.org/the-narrative-in-a-suitcase-project/

50   https://dulwichcentre.com.au/narratives-in-the-suitcase-by-ncazelo-ncube-mlilo/

51   For more, visit https://dulwichcentre.com.au/courses/maps-of-narrative-practice/lessons/welcome-to-the-maps-of-narrative-practice-course/

52   https://dulwichcentre.com.au/the-tree-of-life/

53   Watch the trailer here https://www.youtube.com/watch?v=f6dKhzYgksc

54   Roman Krznaric "A Handbook for Revolution: Empathy"

55   https://www.linkedin.com/in/sarah-bayliss-42a934a/

56   Be One, Get One: The Importance Of Mentorship, Oct 2 2018. *Forbes*. https://www.forbes.com/councils/yec/2018/10/02/be-one-get-one-the-importance-of-mentorship/

57   Gen X-plore: Three Quarters of Over 50s Seek Career Change to Facilitate Travel Plans, September 9, 2024. https://stories.hilton.com/emea/releases/three-quarters-of-over-50s-seek-career-change-to-facilitate-travel-plans

58   "I've applied for over 300 jobs in the past year—at 58 you don't get a look in" 26 October 2024. *The Telegraph*. https://www.telegraph.co.uk/education-and-careers/2024/10/26/ageism-recruitment-over-50

59   Chimamanda Ngozi Adichie (2009, July). The danger of a single story [Video]. TED Conferences

60   Postructuralism and narrative therapy—what's it all about? Leonie Thomas c/o Dulwich Centre Publications, 2002.

61   Source: McGonigal, Kelly (2015, May) How to make stress your friend [Video]. TED Conferences

62   Beck, Martha (2001), Finding your north star, London, Piatkus Books

63   Boroditsky, Lera (2017, November). How language shapes the way we think [Video]. TED Conferences

64   Swing Time 1936

65   Instagram jane.and.fonda

About the author

Sarah Bird is a professional business writer and editor with more than 30 years of experience in large corporate organisations. Resilience has fuelled her freelance career and led her to write and coach training programmes for post-education jobseekers and students in education to help them reignite or kick-start their careers. For more on storytelling at work, visit https://www.nynclub.co.uk.

in https://www.linkedin.com/in/sarah-bird-4683145/

Printed in Great Britain
by Amazon